819   99₁₀

GW00370546

HERBS

HERBS

Barbara Hey

Illustrations by Nicolette Hey

NEW
HOLLAND

First published in the UK in 1992 by
New Holland (Publishers) Ltd
37 Connaught Street, London W2 2AZ

Copyright © in text and illustrations Barbara Hey
Copyright © New Holland (Publishers) Ltd

All rights reserved.
No part of this publication may be reproduced,
stored in a retrieval system, or transmitted,
in any form or by any means, electronic, mechanical,
photocopying, recording or otherwise, without the prior
written permission of the copyright owner and publishers.

ISBN 1 85368 151 2

Editor: Laura van Niekerk
Designer: Abdul Amien
Phototypeset by Diatype Setting cc
Reproduction by Unifoto (Pty) Ltd
Printed and bound in Singapore by Kyodo Printing Co (Pte) Ltd

CONTENTS

PREFACE

This book stems from my love of gardening, in particular herbs, instilled in me at an early age by my mother, a wonderful, instinctive gardener. I hope that some of the knowledge I have gained over many years will create a lasting interest in the growing, identifying and using of herbs for the novice gardener, and that the seasoned gardener will gather some new insights into this fascinating way of life.

This is in no way meant to be a complete or botanical book of herbs as I have only dealt with some of the plants which are of most use and should be freely available from friends or nurseries. As space and time permits you will, like me, find yourself investigating many more species and varieties. Find people who are already growing herbs and you will make new friends as herbs bring people together.

Because of the importance of herbs since time long past, I have included something of their history, origin and ancient uses. I have also drawn from the old works of herbalists such as Culpeper, Gerard and Parkinson, who in turn drew knowledge from the ancients who on occasion used 'kill or cure' methods to discover the curative properties of some herbs.

My granddaughter, Nicolette, because of her feel for growing things learnt from her mother, has done the paintings and drawings for this book from life. It has taken a great deal of patience and ability since seasonal fluctuations have caused flowers and plants to not always be at their best when needed. Robert, my elder grandson, has had the task of sorting Gran's manuscript and translating it into computer-readable material. Their brother, Charles, with his zany sense of humour, has saved the day on occasions when we all got a little uptight. To them my loving thanks for making this writing a pleasure. To my many herb-growing friends for their advice and help so willingly given, thank you.

BARBARA M. HEY
THE HERB HOUSE
APRIL 1992

❛ *Talke of perfect happinesse or pleasure, and what place was so fit for that as the garden place where Adam was set to be the Herbalist.* ❜

John Gerard

I always feel that gardening should be a pleasure, not a chore, and if at all possible one should do the planting and maintaining oneself; untrained help can mean death to a garden, especially where herbs are grown. The self-sown treasures which act as fillers in many gardens, sometimes growing into mature plants, often simply disappear unnoticed among the weeds. And many of these so-called weeds are in fact valuable herbs; only the sensitive gardener knowing when to thin out, leave alone or discard.

I started working in my mother's garden from an early age and have had my own gardens for over 45 years. The first gardens were made up of what was to start with, grey, seaside-like sand which has a very high silicon content, causing water to run off rather than sink in. In fact this is so high that the sand is mined and exported for the manufacture of glass!

To make this and any other type of difficult soil arable, it is necessary to build it up with well-rotted manure and compost and more compost and manure. Inorganic fertilizers tend to leach through the ground rapidly and therefore their effectiveness is short-lived. Hoof and horn, bonemeal (the mineral content of these two being different), milled seaweed and liquid fish and seaweed sprays are excellent for feeding the soil.

If 'yellowing' of the foliage occurs, particularly with sandy soil, the simplest treatment is a solution of two tablespoons Epsom salts, (magnesium sulphate), dissolved in 5 ℓ/600 fl oz of water, either used as a foliar spray or watered around the plant. If this does not work, try iron chelate or a proprietary trace element mix. Herbs usually prefer an alkaline soil so if need be, add some agricultural lime. Plants in containers may benefit from some extra liquid feeding, but don't overdo this.

A useful tip to aid water retention in sandy soil is to keep the beds lower than the surrounding paths and grass areas. If the beds are banked and dry, the water rolls off before it can soak in.

Formal herb gardens need a great deal of time and attention and unless there is enough space, one is limited in the varieties one can grow. Small, neat hedges for edging are not always successful as they tend to grow too fast in temperate climates.

An informal garden can give unexpected pleasure as all is not revealed at once and the special needs of individual plants can be met. Herbs can be grown among other garden plants in a shrubbery or bed for a contrast in textures and colours in the foliage and flowers. For small gardens, patios or where the ground is not suitable near the kitchen, pots and other containers come into their own. Try stacking them for even more growing space.

As one gets older or as disabilities set in, there is often no need to give up the pleasure of growing herbs. Raised growing areas, high containers and windowsills eliminate the need for bending or kneeling. Look out for garden tools that have been adapted to special needs, and cushioned kneeling frames which facilitate getting up from and down to earth level. A lightweight wheelbarrow also makes gardening easier. Remember, the older one gets the more minerals, trace elements and vitamins are needed which are so easily obtained from a few fresh, home-grown herbs.

Plant pests and diseases should not present difficulties, provided the correct ecological balance is maintained. Never use commercial pesticides or herbicides in a herb garden or any other garden for that matter. In the six years that I have been in my present suburban garden, I have achieved a perfect ecological balance. I water the herbs – there are some 350 varieties – by hand, in this way keeping a constant watch for garden pests such as aphids and scale which, if caught early, can be simply rubbed off by hand. Aphids can also be sprayed with a jet of cold water or a soapy water mix. Mealy bug and scale can be brushed off with an old toothbrush dipped in a mixture of half methylated spirits to half water. Grasshoppers and other large insects can be squashed or beheaded; caterpillars are moved into the hedge or squashed, and snails are dropped into a bucket of strong lime or salt water. A dusting of tobacco dust will also protect your seedlings from the small conical snail. As Alan Walker said : 'They who hold the hose, know their garden.'

In an ecologically-balanced garden, you might be surprised, as I was, by the return of a family of small russet snakes and hitherto unseen bird species, all of which do wonders in keeping the pest and snail population down.

English mint

Remember also that certain birds, toads, frogs, especially bullfrogs, chameleons, praying mantises, spiders, snakes, lizards and fat earthworms all have their place in a natural, healthy garden.

When I took over the property, which is now known as the 'Herb House', the only things growing were a very mixed hedge on the one side, and an old, spreading English mulberry tree, (*Morus nigra*). Today the garden is lush and interesting, although not always neat and tidy.

Feel the peace of mind that working in a garden gives and take time to look around, breathe deeply of the fragrances and enjoy life.

❧*Heaven is not only above your head, it is under your feet as well.*❧

Thoreau

GROWING HERBS

Layering

Layering is a method of propagating without removing a stem from the mother plant before it has rooted. Take a low-growing stem or branch, gently crack or cut it half-way through and place it in the soil close to the mature plant. Cover it with soil and peg it down or place a stone or piece of brick over the break to keep it firmly in position.

Water the plant in the usual way, but do not disturb it for about six weeks. Then carefully remove the restraints and check for rooting. If a good root system has developed, sever the stem from the main plant and let it grow in a bag or pot of compost-rich soil until it has sufficiently developed to be moved to a more permanent position in the garden.

Cuttings or 'slips'

For successful propagation of cuttings you require fairly shallow boxes or trays of river sand, or clean sand purloined from a building site. You also need a general purpose hormone rooting powder and a piece of dowel or anything else suitable for making holes in the sand. Always have a can of water handy and keep everything together in a shady spot near the house. This way it will be easy to plant cuttings as soon as they are cut or are brought home and you won't lose any by leaving them to rot in water on the windowsill.

Take cuttings as follows: Always take them below a node. Strip the surplus foliage and any buds from cuttings and if the stems are woody, scrape the base lightly. Dip them in water, shake and then dip them in rooting powder before you insert them in holes made in sand trays. Place the cuttings close together to save space and to accelerate root growth. Firm them down and keep the soil damp but not overwatered. In six weeks time, carefully loosen the sand. If the cuttings are well-rooted, lift them gently and continue to grow them in bags of compost-rich soil until they are mature enough to plant in the garden. Cuttings propagated in this way develop good root systems

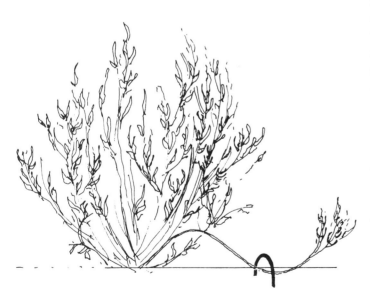

that search for nourishment in the sand and once they are well-fed in composted soil, will thrive. Keep in mind that soft, succulent stems will do much better without rooting powder.

Growing herbs in pots

Drainage is all-important and to ensure proper drainage, place broken crocks or china at the bottom of the pot over the drainage holes. Use compost-rich, light soil to which bonemeal has been added.

Pots are very convenient in that they take up little space and can be moved around to catch maximum sunlight as needed. Mints especially should be confined to containers as most varieties are invasive. Other herbs that will do well in pots or containers are rosemary, pennyroyal, chives, parsley and catmint.

Making compost

Well-made compost is essential for good gardens; it provides trace elements and nutriment and prevents excessive leaching and drying out of the soil. It also helps to bind sandy soil and break up heavy clay soil.

A compost heap can be made by combining biodegradable kitchen waste, bits of newspaper, recycled egg boxes, wine bottle sleeves, lawn cuttings, garden clippings, weeds, manure, sand and activating herbs. Numbered among the best activating herbs are comfrey, yarrow, tansy, dandelion and nettle. Surplus plants or a small bunch of leaves of any one variety are all that is needed.

Make a neat heap of the collected material or pack it in a wire netting enclosure, spreading manure (any kind) evenly between layers, making sure to place the activating herb or herbs in the centre. Lawn cuttings should not be allowed to stay in a mass but must be well interspersed. Dampen the material lightly as you work, pressing it down firmly and finally covering it with a layer of sand.

To prevent my garden beds from becoming too high, I remove some of the subsoil before adding compost and making a new planting. In this way there is usually sand available for the next compost covering.

Do not allow the heap to dry out. At the end of the first week, insert a metal rod into the centre of the heap and leave it there for five minutes. When removed, the tip

should feel hot. This will mean that the compost is working well and the heat should destroy weed seeds etc. After six weeks, turn and repack the heap to introduce more oxygen. In summer the compost should be ready at the end of a further six weeks. In winter it will take longer.

Cover your heap with plastic sheeting to prevent it from getting too wet when it rains. When you start breaking down the heap to use the compost in the garden, remove any undecomposed material to add to the next heap.

A word of advice: be careful not to include vegetable peelers, kitchen knives and small garden tools in the compost material, it doesn't do them much good.

The best time to cut herbs for drying is mid-morning on a warm, clear day when the early morning moisture has dissipated and the sun is not yet hot enough to draw off the volatile oils. If a quantity is to be cut and dried for culinary use, hose the herbs down the night before so that they will be free of dust.

Plant material suitable for bunching can be tied firmly in loose bundles and hung in the shade or in the dark in a dry area. A garage, however, won't be suitable because of the exhaust fumes.

If you start collecting seeds from bunches, cover the bunches with paper bags punctured for ventilation. Single flowers, loose petals and foliage can be spread on newspaper or wire mesh trays away from sunlight.

Lavender and other herbs of which the flowering stems and upper plant leaves are used, are best cut when the first flowers open. Foliage herbs, such as thyme, basil, sage, mint, lemon balm, celery and lovage are best cut before flowering when the oils are at their strongest. When collecting flowers of yarrow and chamomile and petals of calendula, take care that they are not bruised or marked and that they are freshly opened.

Collect seeds before they fall to the ground, when they are almost ripe, by cutting the whole stem and inverting the head of seeds into a paper bag.

Before storing your harvested herbs in dry, airtight glass jars or using them in potpourri and pillows, take care that all the herbs are completely dry to the touch. A few slightly damp pieces can cause mould and spoil the result of your hard work.

❦ The seed is that part of the plant which is endowed with a vital faculty to bring forth its like, and it contains potentially the whole plant in it. ❦

Culpeper

USING HERBS

Tussie mussie

A tussie mussie is a bouquet of fresh herbs originally carried in the 1300s to ward off the Black Death. In later years judges and magistrates in England held them to their noses (hence the name nosegays) to lessen the smell of convicts brought up from the dungeons and cells, and to this day, on special occasions, English judges in robes and wigs may be seen carrying tussie mussies. When Queen Elizabeth II entered Westminster Abbey for her coronation she also had a herb bouquet and during Victorian times, these fragrant posies were used as a means of communication between lovers, each herb conveying a special message for example violets for faithfulness and lemon balm for sympathy.

Nowadays we make them as gifts for friends in need of cheer and for hostesses as tokens of thanks. They keep well for about a week if the water is kept fresh. The stems should then be mopped dry and the posy hung upside down until crisply dry. Hang tussie mussies in your wardrobe or cupboard for fragrance.

To make a tussie mussie you will need the following:

- a roll of green florist's tape
- a pair of sharp scissors
- a pair of secateurs
- pretty ribbon — waterproof or florist's
- a thin rubber band
- a small glass jar or vase
- a lacy paper posy holder (optional)

Pick a medium-sized rosebud or open carnation. Select eight or ten each of about seven or eight different varieties of herb, such as the various lavenders, grey lavender foliage and cotton lavender foliage and buds. Variegated applemint, marjoram or oreganum buds or flowers, and rosemary will also do fine, whereas fennel, parsley and celery flowers and some gypsophila will all give a soft effect. In fact, any sweet-smelling plant material that dries well will be suitable.

Cut the stems to about 12 cm/5 in in length and allow to stand in water for a while. Then carefully strip the stems of foliage, leaving at least 4 cm/1½ in of growth at the tip. Spread the strippings on the floor on some newspaper to dry for your potpourri.

Cut 4–5 cm/1½–2 in pieces of florist's tape on the slant. Select two or three stems of herb, for example one rosemary, one lavender head and one marjoram, and tape them together. Do the same with the other herbs, this will make it easier to handle them. Bind four or five small rose geranium leaves around the rosebud to form the centre and continue taping the small bundles evenly in circles around the bud. Intersperse with soft flowers of fennel, parsley, celery or gypsophila. The last circle should be of long English lavender heads and cotton lavender foliage. Surround the whole with a few large rose or peppermint geranium leaves, taping them firmly. Trim the stems and slip on the rubber band to hold everything together as the stems tend to shrink as they dry.

If you are going to use a posy holder, slip it on at this stage. Neaten with tape and tie your ribbon over this, leaving the ends and part of the bow to show above the flowers. Place the tussie mussie in a small jar or vase of water.

Of leaves choose only such as are green and full of juice; pick them carefully and cast away such as are declining, for they will putrify the rest. So shall one handful be worth ten of those you buy in Cheapside.

Culpeper

Potpourri

Making a potpourri is very simple. Start by collecting some pretty flowers, they do not all have to be perfumed. When picking roses, include some of the foliage – the dry leaves add good colour. You will need plenty of sweet foliage herbs like geranium, lemon verbena, melissa, mints, etc. Anti-moth herbs like cotton lavender, southernwood, tansy and so forth can be used in potpourri bags for wardrobes and cupboards, and for a more spicy mix, try combining dry basil, bay, oreganum and sweet marjoram. Cloves, cinnamon, cardamom and nutmeg will all make good additions to any potpourri.

You will need fixatives, and for this orris root powder, minced and pounded flag iris rhizomes and vetiver root, seed of clary sage and minced citrus peel can be used. The least expensive and most readily available is dry citrus peel, complete with pith, minced and slowly dried on trays in the sun or a cool oven.

Lastly you need a few good oils. Lavender, rose, lemon or orange are among the most versatile to start with. As the best oils are expensive, use with a light hand.

Depending on what you have harvested, dry the foliage and flowers on sheets of newspaper or hang in bunches until just crisp. And now to mix: Spread a piece of sheeting on the floor, strip and discard any hard stems and blend the material in the rough proportion of a generous handful of citrus peel to four cups of plant material and about half a teaspoon of oils. Stir well with your hands, then pack firmly into an airtight container (not tin). Use a plastic bag and tie tightly if you have nothing else suitable.

Leave your mix like this for a few days and then tip it out onto some sheeting to test the perfume. Make adjustments if needed and without washing it, fold your sheet up for next time. Store the potpourri in pretty jars, taking the lids off when you want the fragrance to fill the room. This potpourri can also be sewn into sachets to be placed in wardrobes, cupboards or drawers.

Herb or sleep pillows

A herb or sleep pillow makes a wonderful gift. Or why not treat yourself to one! Here's how to make it. Make a pillow liner of fine cotton material and stuff it with suitable fragrant sleep-inducing herbs, such as well-dried basil, lemon balm, chamomile, hops, lavender, marjoram, peppermint, sage, woodruff, thyme, catnip and rose petals. If you prefer a softer pillow, mix the herbs with silk cotton or synthetic cushion filler. A few drops of fragrant oils and spices like aniseed may be added to mixtures. Mind not to overstuff the pillow.

Finish the pillow off by stitching it into an attractive cover, made from lace, candlewick, broderie anglaise or other pretty materials.

❛*A bag to smell unto for melancholy*
or to cause one to sleep
and is good to smell
unto at other times.❜

William Ram

15

Crystallizing flowers and leaves

Select the most perfect violet and borage flowers, large rose petals and mint leaves. These all make edible and attractive decorations for cakes, desserts, mousses and ice creams.

The simplest method is to lightly beat an egg white (not stiff). Then, with a small, firm, bristled brush, lightly coat each petal and leaf with egg white, before dusting thoroughly with castor sugar. Shake off the surplus sugar and arrange carefully on waxed paper on trays. If the sun is very hot on that day, you can dry them outside, otherwise in a warming oven until firm and crisp. Store in airtight jars in layers separated by wax paper and hide from children who delight in these dainties.

A slightly more complicated method involves dissolving 30 g/1 oz of gum arabic in 300 ml/10 fl oz hot water. When it has cooled down, dip the flowers and leaves in one at a time and shake gently, removing any surplus fluid. Dust with castor sugar and proceed as above.

❧ *Sound savorie, and brazil, hartie-hale*
Fat Colwortes and comforting Perseline,
Cold Lettuce and refreshing Rosmarine.❧

Lady Northcote

Herb tea

A herb tea is a simple tea made by picking the herb or herbs of your choice, putting them in a mug or china teapot, and pouring boiling water over. When cooled to a drinkable temperature, a little honey and/or lemon juice may be added to enhance or disguise the flavour. Some herb teas also make a refreshing drink when served chilled. And if your tea needs a extra touch of colour or flavour, add some rosehip or herb tea. But remember, if you are not absolutely certain about identifying a herb, it would be wiser to buy the dried herb from a reputable health shop.

❧ *Let food be your medicine*
and medicine your food.❧

Hippocrates

Herb vinegars and oils

Why not add some life to ordinary vinegar and oil used in everyday cooking? It is simple and all you need is a herb or couple of herbs of your choice. Experiment with combinations of oreganum, nasturtium and rosemary for potency and use chives, marjoram, geranium and thyme for milder flavours. French tarragon can be a temperamental plant to grow, but if you are lucky enough to find some, it makes an excellent vinegar.

For oil, sunflower oil will do and for vinegar, choose grape, apple cider or your own preferred make. Do not use blended vinegars, though, they tend to be very harsh.

Then you will also need a wide-mouthed glass jar and a sheet of plastic wrap to cover its top. I find lids spoil with oil and vinegar.

Pick your herbs, wash them and pat or swing dry in a tea towel. Pack the jar ¾ full and top up with vinegar or oil. Seal the top with plastic wrap and stand the jar in full sun in a meadow or on a windowsill for about a week. Then strain through butter muslin or a thoroughly clean nylon stocking, squeezing out the last drop. If you find the flavour not strong enough, repeat with some fresh herbs, using the same oil or vinegar and topping up if necessary.

Strain carefully and pour into attractive bottles, finishing off with a suitable sprig for decoration. Write out pretty labels and you will have most appreciated gifts.

❦Better is a dinner of herbs where love is, than a stalled ox and hatred therewith.❧

Proverbs

*❦Speak not — whisper not;
Here bloweth thyme and bergamot;
Softly on the evening hour,
Secret herbs their spices shower.
Dark-spiked rosemary and myrrh,
Lean-stalked, purple lavender;
Hides within her bosom, too,
All her sorrows, bitter rue.❧*

Walter de la Mare

Bath oils

Bath oils need no longer be a once-a-month luxury. You can make your own by using technical oil (cosmetic oil), obtainable from chemists, and relax in a fragrant, nourishing bath every day of the week. Make it exactly as you would culinary oils (*see* above), though you would in this instance choose herbs for their strong perfume content, rather than flavour. Rosemary, lavender, lemon verbena, lemon balm, mint and scented geraniums all make lovely bath oils.

❦But those which perfume the Aire most delightfully, not passed by as the rest, but being Trodden upon and Crushed, are Three: That is, Burnet, Wilde-Time, and Water-Mints. Therefore, you are to set whole Allies of them, to have the Pleasure, when you walke or tread.❧

Francis Bacon

BASIL

Ocimum basilicum

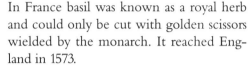

asil is a historical herb that has been used for thousands of years. Its name is derived from the Greek *basilikos*, meaning royal. It is a tropical herb, presumably brought from Persia to Greece by Alexander the Great, from where it soon reached Italy, becoming an essential herb in their cooking. In Greece, basil is a symbol of misfortune and poverty, yet in yet in Italy it symbolizes love. Funnily enough, both in Athens and Rome it was thought that the plant would not grow unless it was verbally abused and sworn at while being sown!

Sweet basil

In France basil was known as a royal herb and could only be cut with golden scissors wielded by the monarch. It reached England in 1573.

A native of India and Asia, it also grows extensively in Egypt and the Middle East where it is considered sacred by Hindus who dedicate it to Vishnu and Krishna. As a ritual they place sprigs of basil in the hands of their dead and plant it on their graves. It is known as 'tulsi' and is grown around temples and houses, sometimes attaining a height of up to 2 m/6 ft 6 in.

Culpeper had no good to say of it, except: 'Being applied to the place bitten by venomous beasts, or stung by a wasp or hornet, it speedily draws the poison out. Every like draws its like.'

Nowadays there are many varieties of basil grown all over the world — the most common are sweet basil, a purple variety called 'dark opal', dwarf basil, tall bush basil and lettuceleaf basil. The dwarf bush and purple basil make attractive borders.

Growing basil

This herb is an annual and grows from seed sown in early summer. Keep in mind that basil seed retains its germinating properties for many years, but tends to hybridize when several varieties are grown in proximity. Plant or sow your basil in the sun or semi-shade, but not near rue, as this herb inhibits its growth. Basil also makes an excellent pot plant and will grow well on a sunny windowsill.

Dark opal

In hot weather, gently hose down the basil plants to revive the tired leaves. When harvesting basil, always leave two leaves or a circle of leaves toward the base of each branch and don't despair; new tops are sure to appear within a week.

Using basil

As basil is best picked fresh, try taking cuttings from unflowered shoots towards the end of summer. The warm, spicy smell and flavour of basil makes it an ideal herb for all tomato dishes, pizza, pasta and salads. It is a classic ingredient of *pesto* (recipe below), which you can make and freeze to use over a variety of pastas or with roast lamb during winter.

Make bottles of basil vinegar and basil oil, adding an extra sprig for decoration (*see* p. 16). For the most part the leaves are used, but I'm constantly nipping off the flowers to promote plant growth and end up using these as well.

Dioscorides warns: 'Eating too much basil weakens the eyesight and is difficult to digest'. The Hindus nevertheless chew it and we actually make a tea with basil to *aid* digestion. The tea made from the flowers has a sedative quality and can also be used as a mouthwash for infected gums and ulcers. Just add six large leaves to a cup of boiling water, leave it for a while to infuse, then rinse the mouth.

Other uses include placing a pot of basil in the kitchen to keep flies away and similarly a few twigs tossed on a *braai* fire will discourage mosquitoes. Dried basil has of course always been a popular potpourri ingredient and is also often used in sleep pillows (*see* p. 17) because of its sedative properties.

❛*Madonna wherefore hast thou sent to me*
Sweet basil and mignonette?
Embleming love and health, which never yet
In the same wreath might be.❜

Percy Bysshe Shelley

To make that classic Italian sauce, *pesto*, purée one cup of washed and dried basil leaves, five or six cloves of garlic, about a quarter cup pine nuts and one cup grated Parmesan cheese with two to three teaspoons of good olive oil. Gradually add a further half cup of olive oil to the blending mix until it emulsifies and season with salt and freshly ground black pepper. Store your *pesto* in a glass jar, pouring a thin layer of olive oil over to seal. Cover the jar tightly and refrigerate or freeze.

You can quite successfully preserve basil if you don't have a continual supply, but be sure to pick the leaves when they are still young. To preserve them you simply paint both sides of the leaves with good olive oil and then freeze them or leave them to dry. You could also store whole leaves with salt in a jar of olive oil or dry-pack them with salt.

When using basil in food, always pound the leaf with oil or tear the leaf with your fingers, rather than attempting to chop the herb.

Lettuceleaf basil

Tall bush basil

Dwarf bush basil

Basil is also known as the tomato herb because it goes so well in all dishes containing tomato. You can make a tasty baked tomato dish with basil by choosing ripe tomatoes, cutting each in half and removing the cores.

Season each with salt and freshly ground black pepper and sprinkle chopped spring onion and shredded, fresh basil leaves over. Dot with butter, arrange in a buttered baking dish and bake in a preheated moderate oven for ten minutes. Brown under a grill for a further three minutes and serve. Delicious!

You can also make a simple tomato and basil salad by cutting some firm tomatoes (say four) crosswise into thin slices and arranging them, overlapping, on a flat dish. Season them well with salt and freshly ground black pepper.

Mix approximately three to four tablespoons olive oil with one teaspoon lemon juice or wine vinegar and sprinkle over the tomatoes.

To finish the salad off, blanch six to eight shallots in boiling water for 30 seconds, refresh them under cold water and drain well. Chop the shallots up and add to that some eight to ten shredded basil leaves. Finally sprinkle the greens over the tomatoes and serve.

●*A certain Gentleman of Siena*
being wonderfully taken and delighted with the
Smell of Basil,
was wont very frequently to take
the Powder of the dry Herb and Snuff it up his Nose;
but in a short Time he turn'd mad and died;
and his Head being opened by Surgeons,
there was found a Nest of Scorpions in his Brain.●

Tournefort

BORAGE

Borago officinalis

(Bee bread)

As a symbol of courage, the simple, brilliant blue flower of borage was embroidered on garments worn by knights going on crusades and today still appears in old embroidery designs. In medieval times wine spiked with borage was often drunk to 'lift the spirits' and it has traditionally been added to drinks and salads for its benefits as an invigorating tonic.

It's a plant loved by and known to encourage bees, hence the old name 'bee bread'.

Borage

Growing borage

Borage is an annual which self-sows throughout the year in temperate areas. Though lax in growth, it grows quite high, and should thus be grown in clumps for self-support. It will take full sun or semi-shade and the richer the soil, the lusher the growth. Thick stems grow from a base of large leaves, all covered in bristly hairs. The flowers are mostly a vivid blue, star-shaped with white-circled black stamens.

Using borage

For use as a cough remedy or blood purifier, cover half a cup of chopped leaves with two and a half cups of boiling water. Made in small quantities and sipped, heated, at bedtime, it also induces sleep. Flowers crystallize well (*see* p. 16) and can be used to decorate cakes and desserts. Used fresh they pretty-up trifles, fruit salads, Pimms No. 1 or white wine. The cucumber flavour of fresh, young leaves lends itself to salads, herb cheese, butter and dips. Slightly more mature leaves can be chopped and added to a variety of dishes, including soups and stews.

❧ *Here is sweet water and borage for blending, Comfort and courage to drink at your will.* ❧

Nora Hopper

COMFREY

Symphytum officinale

(Knitbone, bruisewort or boneset)

The name comfrey comes from the Latin *confervére*, which means to grow together. Comfrey earned this name through its medieval reputation of being able to join broken bones. In joining the limbs, a plaster was made by grating the comfrey root, mixing it to a mash with a little water, then leaving it to set on the limb.

Comfrey has a thick root stock, producing broad basal leaves in a fountain-like formation. The leaves are somewhat hairy, though finer than those of borage. Heads of drooping flowers appear, shading from white to blue to purple, depending on the variety.

Growing comfrey

Comfrey is a perennial herb, but in some areas it does, however, die down in winter. The plants will grow well in sun or semi-shade in rich, moist soil. Propagate by root division or root cuttings (*see* p. 10) and watch out for snails, slugs and caterpillars. In autumn, a light dressing of lime will do the plant good and help it survive.

Using comfrey

Comfrey is an important compost activator (*see* p. 11) and is valued as a liquid fertilizer for its high potash content. Allow some leaves to rot in water, strain and spray the liquid on plants. It is grown as a fodder crop in Britain, North America, Kenya and Japan and is an ideal additive to poultry, pig and horse feeds.

Comfrey has a high protein content and is rich in vitamin B12, thus making it an important addition to vegetarian diets. Allantoin, a healing agent, is one of the active components of comfrey and is found to be more concentrated in the root than the leaf.

When the young leaves are cooked in butter or with cabbage or other green vegetables, the hairiness disappears.

Taken with discretion in the form of tea or a tablet, it speeds the healing of broken bones and certain forms of rheumatism and arthritis respond to a course of treatment. Poultices can be applied to swollen joints to alleviate inflammation and leg ulcers and bed sores will respond to comfrey in an aqueous cream base.

*Though rumours exist that the alkaloid in comfrey might be toxic, this has been proven to be incorrect through extensive research by three prominent institutions in Britain.

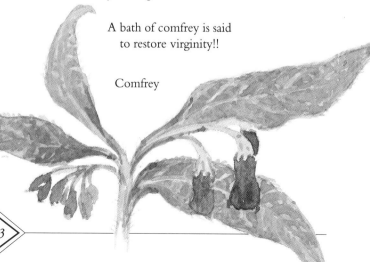

A bath of comfrey is said to restore virginity!!

Comfrey

DANDELION

This herb, named by the French 'dent de lion', originally came from Europe and Asia and must have got its name from the shape of the leaves, which do bear some resemblance to lion's teeth. In Culpeper's time it was sometimes called 'Piss-a-beds', presumably referring to its diuretic qualities.

The dandelion must not be confused with the tough bitter weed so often found in lawns. The true dandelion has a fleshy root from which come deeply scalloped leaves forming a low crown near the ground. Upright stems produce clear, yellow daisy-like flowers which in turn become round fluffy seed heads. If you have to control the spread of the plant, cut the heads off before they float away.

Growing dandelion

Although a perennial herb, dandelion is usually grown as an annual. It prefers open, sunny spots — the flowers refuse to open in the shade — and rich, loamy soil. Generally it looks after itself, but would appreciate some water in dry weather.

❛ *Shock-headed Dandelion*
That drank the fire of the sun ❜

Robert Bridges

Using dandelion

Early references in 10th century Arabic writings prized it for its medicinal properties, and today research is being done into how it can be used in measured dosage for various complaints.

Old writings keep repeating that it is good for treating liver diseases, but they are vague as to exactly how. It is a good diuretic and also makes an excellent tonic. Apparently the juice is effective used on warts.

Dandelion is highly nutritious, containing vitamins and minerals, particularly vitamin A and magnesium, the latter being especially helpful in preventing those agonizing leg cramps. For a blood purifier, simmer 30 g/1 oz of dried root in two cups of water for ten minutes — *do not boil*. Strain, refrigerate and take a sherry glassful once a day.

Dandelion

The root of a well-grown plant, washed, minced, roasted and processed in a coffee grinder, makes excellent caffeine-free coffee, or can be added to coffee in place of chicory. Fresh roots can also be washed, sliced and added to soups and stews just as one would parsnips. Young leaves can be torn and added to salads and sandwiches, cooked with other vegetables or prepared like spinach. If you find the leaves too bitter, pre-soak them in salted water for about 30 minutes, rinse and dry.

Both the leaves and flowers can be used to make a delicious dandelion wine, and the leaves are known to make good dandelion stout. You can make your own, refreshing dandelion wine that is also an excellent tonic as follows: Place about ten handfuls of dandelion flowers, picked early in the morning, in a bowl and cover them with water. Leave to stand for 3 days, stirring the flowers occasionally. Strain, discard the flowers and boil the liquid for half an hour. Add 625 g/22 oz sugar and the rind and the juice of 2 lemons and 1 orange. Stir one teaspoon of yeast into some warm water and add this to the dandelion mixture. Pour the liquid into a fermenting jar and leave for about 2 months before you bottle the wine.

Dandelion buds, gently cooked in butter, add a lovely taste to an omelette; use approximately one quarter cup of buds to two eggs. When sufficient flowers are available they make a delicious wine. In short, dandelion is a wonderful, useful 'weed'.

❧Dandelion this
A college youth that flashes for a day
All gold; anon he doffs his goudy suit,
Touch'd by the magic hand of some grave Bishop
And all at once, by commutation strange,
Becomes a Reverend Divine❧

James Hurdis *The Village Curate*

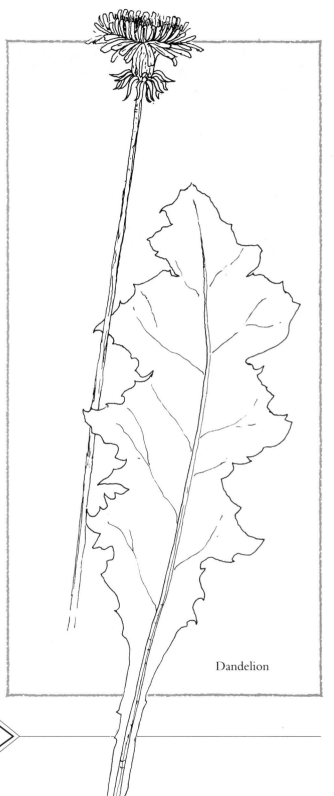

Dandelion

CHIVES

Allium schoenoprasum

(Old English chives, civet, sweth, rush leeks)

The humble chive is amongst the oldest recorded herbs, going back almost 5000 years, and is also one of the best-known culinary herbs. Today one rarely finds chives in the wild. It is a beautiful edging to any garden and because it grows from its base, as does grass, you can cut and come again. Belonging to the onion family, as does the leek, garlic and shallot, it is a bulb with long hairlike roots which sprout hollow grey-green, grasslike stems. In mid-summer tight heads of pink to purple flowers will appear that can be cut to keep the plant strong. I like to keep some flowers for the kitchen or as cut flowers in the home.

Chives

Growing chives

Generally clumps of chives grown in borders or pots will take some shade, but full sun is essential to prevent the plant from dying back in winter. For healthy chives, feed the soil with rotted manure and a liquid organic fertilizer and after a few years, when the clumps become too tight, lift and divide the plants. If growing in pots, these can be narrow, but must be deep as the roots are long.

Scissors are the best for harvesting and cutting up — chopping can make a mush. Leave at least 5 cm/2 in of stem and cut only half of a clump at one time.

Using chives

Chives have little medicinal use, though their mildly antiseptic qualities may have some healing effect.

They are best used fresh when cooking, and add flavour to salads, soups, egg dishes, sauces and cream cheese mixtures. Add some flowers to white wine vinegar for a delicately flavoured, pinkish vinegar that not only looks good, but tastes wonderful.

They are indeed a kind of leeks, hot and dry in the fourth degree, and so under the dominations of Mars . . . if they be eaten raw they send up very hurtful vapours to the brain causing troublesome sleep and spoiling the eyesight.

Culpeper

GARLIC CHIVES

Allium tuberosum

(Chinese chives)

These chives with their wonderful garlic flavour differ in appearance from common chives in that their leaves are flatter and wider, growing from small rhizomes. They often die back in winter, but mark the place of planting and expect them to reappear in summer.

Growing garlic chives

Garlic chives grow quite happily in pots, but still need lots of sun and should be kept damp. Their seeds germinate well and when the plants are a reasonable size, can be planted out about 25 cm/10 in from each other. The attractive, white flowers grow in starlike clusters on long slender stems and are very fragrant. Garlic chives can be harvested in a similar manner to common chives.

Using garlic chives

This delicious herb is widely used in Chinese cooking, hence the name 'Chinese chives'. Keep in mind that it has a more pungent flavour though, and a little goes along way.

It can be used as an excellent salt substitute for chicken, pork and lamb dishes and can be frozen successfully. Make tasty garlic chive butter by creaming 4 tablespoons of chopped garlic chives and 100g/4 oz butter. Beat in 1 tablespoon of lemon juice, adding salt and black pepper to taste. Garlic chives are also reputed to enhance the scent of roses when planted near them.

❛*And, most dear actors, eat no onions nor garlic, for we are to utter sweet breath.*❜

Shakespeare

Garlic chives

GARLIC
Allium sativum

The growing and use of garlic goes back to 2000 B.C., where it was first used on the Steppes of Djungar, in Kirghiz and central Asia.

Garlic, first grown in England in 1540, was known as 'poorman's treacle', treacle coming from 'theriac', meaning 'cure-all'. The name garlic is derived from the Old English words *gar* (lance) and *leac* (leek), referring to the spear-like shape of the leaves, cloves and stem. An old Muslim legend has it that garlic came into the world on Satan's left foot and onion on his right — which should say something of its potency!

Today garlic is a growing ingredient of cooking all over the world and is medicinally still held in high regard.

Growing garlic

Garlic is grown from large cloves, divided and planted in full sun under light, well-drained, composted soil. The cloves, usually planted in autumn, can take up to nine months to mature.

❧ *Sith Garlicke then hath power to save from death,*
Beare with it though it makes unsavory breath;
And scorne not Garlicke, like to some that think
It onely makes men winke, and drinke, and stinke. ❧

John Harrington

Using garlic

The young foliage can be chopped and added to salads or omelettes, but it's the clove that is so much favoured in cooking. It adds wonderful flavour, whilst being rich in minerals and vitamins A, B, and C.

To help sweeten the breath after eating garlic, chew parsley, mint or sage.

In Britain during the Middle Ages it was used to cure various ills, amongst which leprosy. Nowadays the bulblet is used in many treatments, from constipation and catarrh to bronchitis, garlic being by far the most beneficial plant for human health.

Garlic

SHALLOT

Allium ascalonium

(French eschalots)

The shallot is considered the most delectable of all onions. It also being ing known as eschalot (Ascalonian onion) stems from when it was brought back by the crusaders from Ascalon, an ancient city in West Palestine, and introduced into England and the Continent.

Growing shallots

The shallot is a perennial bulb which divides into segments as it grows. It forms hollow, green, onion-like leaves which grow to about 30 cm/12 in. It will need composted soil and to be fed with well-rotted manure.

You can pull clumps of shallots from the ground as you need them. Come winter, the leaves will yellow and once they are shrivelled, the bulbs can be lifted and left in the sun to dry. They can then be stored in a cool, dry place for use in cooking or for the next spring planting.

Using shallots

Shallots have a delicate flavour and when cooked in butter should only be softened and not browned, as this makes them bitter. The tops and bulbs can be used raw and are excellent in salads, omelettes and sandwich fillings. Keep in mind that shallots also make a good pickle, especially with the addition of a few nasturtium seeds.

❝Let onion atoms lurk within the bowl And, half suspected, animate the whole.❞

Sydney Smith

Shallot

29

ORIGANUM

Origanum spp.

There are more than 25 species of *Origanum*, most of which are hardy herbaceous perennials that are loosely (and often incorrectly) referred to as marjorams. For the most part they are natives of the Mediterranean region where the Greeks planted them on graves to ensure the peace and happiness of the dead. Oreganum was in fact called 'Joy of the mountains', derived from *oros* meaning mountain, and *ganos*, joy and beauty. The Greeks also believed marjoram was created by Aphrodite and, like the Romans, they used it in wreaths to crown bridal couples.

In Britain, prior to the use of hops, this herb was used in the brewing of ale. Of this Gerard writes:

> The leaves boiled in water and the decoction drunk easeth such as are given to overmuch singing.

Today there exists a lot of confusion as to the correct naming of oreganums and marjorams, and because of this, I rather describe the herbs as they are commonly known and obtainable from nurseries, with the correct botanical name in italics.

CREEPING GOLDEN MARJORAM

Oreganum aureum

This is truly a beautiful herb and an asset to any garden. Though it has no medicinal or culinary use, it is excellent planted as a ground cover or on banks and walls. The slightly hairy leaves are a dappled green and gold, sometimes all gold, and the dainty flowers are pink.

Creeping golden marjoram

SWEET MARJORAM

Origanum majorana
(Knot marjoram)

This is the herb, known as 'swete margerome' by old her-balists, that Perdita mixes with lavender, mints and savory in *The Winter's Tale* and was used, as Parkinson tells: 'to please the outward senses in nosegays and in the windows of houses, as also in sweete powders, sweete bags, and sweete washing waters'.

Although it was once used medicinally for a number of complaints, it was also highly valued for its disinfectant qualities as a strewing herb on the floors of houses and, re-markably enough, as a meat preserver.

It is a small, woody shrub with soft stems bearing delicate green oval leaves, the clusters of knot-like buds producing fine white flowers. This herb is easily recognized by its distinctive sweet smell and can be grown successfully in containers.

Growing sweet marjoram

It will easily grow to a height of 50 cm/20 in and though it will take some shade, sweet marjoram should be planted in full sun in average soil.

Using sweet marjoram

Both the leaves and flowering tips are used in the home. Sweet marjoram, being a mild, sweet herb, goes well with eggs, fish, chicken and cottage cheese. It can also success-fully be added to a mixed herb tea and will dry well for use in potpourri and herb pillows (*see* p. 15).

To make a tea that will comfort sore throats and at the same time serve as a diuretic, use one tablespoon of fresh herb to a large cup of boiling water. Marjoram of course also makes lovely herb vinegar (*see* p. 16).

I once read that the Greeks crushed the roots for per-fume: 'with lasting scent that women require'. Sounds interesting!

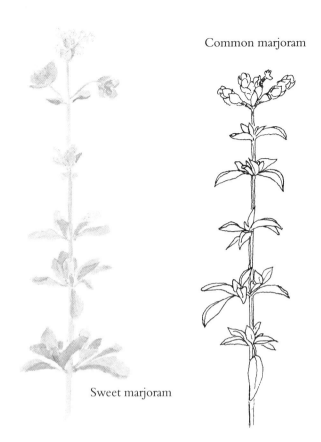

Common marjoram

Sweet marjoram

❧*Indeed, Sir, She was the sweet marjoram*
of the Salad,
or rather the herb of grace.❧

Shakespeare *All's Well that Ends Well*

POT OREGANUM

Origanum onites
(Pot Marjoram)

This variety is a low-growing, good border plant with dark green heart-shaped leaves on purple-tinged stems, produc-ing pale pink flowers. The flavour, though a bit stronger, is similar to common oreganum and the herb is used in the same way.

COMMON OREGANUM

Origanum vulgare
(*Wild marjoram*)

If you want to distinguish this oreganum from the others, look for wiry stems and medium-green, slightly pointed leaves. The herb also sends out roots which produce sturdy clumps that can be detached from the main plant. The flavour is robust and spicy; the leaves are far more pungent and hot than those of sweet marjoram, so use sparingly.

In England it was long esteemed as a medicinal herb, applied as a remedy for coughs and bronchial complaints.

Many confuse oreganum with oregano, the latter being a mixture of mainly *Origanum* species and used as seasoning, especially over Italian dishes.

Pot oreganum

Growing oreganum

Oreganum generally grows to about 60 cm/24 in, producing paired leaves and rosy-pink flowers. The flavour depends to a great extent on the climate and habitat, but for best results oreganum should be planted in a hot, sunny position in average soil. Keep the soil well-drained and cut the plant back to encourage new leaf growth.

Propagation should be from root division, cuttings or layering (*see* p. 10) in spring, though some varieties self-seed and are known to hybridize. To ensure that you have continuous use of your plants, nip off the top shoots from time to time and harvest the leaves for drying before the plant flowers.

Using oreganum

Both pot oreganum and common oreganum are extensively used, fresh or dried, in cooking, especially by the Italians, Portuguese and Greeks. It does wonders for tomato cookery and is delicious used with veal and beef, in mushroom dishes and in a cream sauce over boiled onions.

The flowers have also long been used fresh in flower arrangements or dried in wreaths and bouquets and the whole plant can be used in potpourri and herb or sleep pillows (*see* p. 14).

❛*Where the bee can suck no honey,
she leaves her sting behind;
and where the bear cannot find origanum
to heal his grief,
he blasteth all other leaves with his breath.*❜

Beaumont and Fletcher

Origanum spp.

❝*And though sweet Marjoram will your garden paint*
With no gay colors, yet preserve the plant,
Whose fragrance will invite your kind regard,
When her known virtues have her worth declared;
On Simonis' shore fair Venus raised the plant,
Which from the Goddess touch derived her scent.❞

René Rapin

CATMINT

Nepeta mussinii

Originally from the Continent and Asia, this variety only reached England in the early 1800s from the Caucasus. Catmint is the common garden species, not to be confused with Catnip opposite.

It is a perennial, low-growing plant, with small-toothed, downy, grey-green leaves. Spikes of blue to mauve flowers create a soft misty look, making catmint a good border plant.

Growing catmint

It is a wonderful herb to plant in pots and hanging baskets as the flower stems fall softly. Planted around roses, it will cut down soil evaporation and discourage garden pests. The 'Six Hill Giant' is a lovely, tall, showy hybrid, well worth looking for.

Propagation can be done in spring from cuttings (*see* p. 10) or by root division. After the herb has flowered, cut it down to a basal clump. Catmint will grow happily if adequately watered and placed in a well-drained, sunny position and might even survive in dry areas.

Catmint

Using catmint

The dried foliage exude a lovely fragrance when used in potpourri and herb or sleep pillows (*see* p. 14).

In France the young leaves and shoots are used in salads and as a seasoning. I don't particularly like it and may I add that at *no time* should the leaves be taken by pregnant women. As a medicine small quantities are quite safe and can be taken as a tea to help break a cold fever. A child with a bed-wetting problem may also be helped by drinking a small cup of weak catmint tea with honey and lemon just before bedtime.

*If you set it, the cats will eat it,
If you sow it, the cats won't know it.*

Old rhyme

Catmint is not quite as attractive to cats as . . .

CATNIP

Nepeta cataria

This herb was first cultivated in England as early as AD 1260 and quickly took to the hedgerows. Compared with catmint, it is the true, original herb so much favoured by cats. It is also known for its long history of medical application, although not so used nowadays.

This plant has larger leaves than catmint; they are somewhat egg-shaped, soft green in colour and far more serrated at the edges.

Catnip

Growing catnip

Catnip is somewhat lax in growth, producing stems of dense white flowers decorated with pink blotches.

You can propagate from cuttings (*see* p. 10) or from seed, though it also tends to self-seed. Catnip enjoys full sun and moist yet well-drained soil. Unfortunately it will not grow under dry conditions and if cultivated in hot areas must be planted in the semi-shade. Cut your plant back to basal clumps after flowering.

Using catnip

This is truly a plant grown by cat lovers. Cats eat the leaves and love to roll on the plants – becoming completely besotted with the odour and more or less destroying the plant in the process. If cats cause too much damage, cover the plant with wire mesh until the new growth is strong. Fabric balls stuffed with dried catnip are favoured playthings for cats. Incidentally, catnip is also known to repel rats from the garden or hen house, or wherever a bunch of it is placed.

Medically speaking, catnip taken as a tea is effective in relieving colds and acts as a mild sedative.

❧ *Cats are much delighted herewith; for the smell of it is so pleasant to them that they rub themselves upon it, and wallow in it, and also feed on the leaves very greedily.* ❧

John Gerard

ELDER

Sambucus nigra

(Elderberry)

The elder is a very old herbal plant, native to Europe, western Asia and North Africa. It is a tree steeped in folklore and has gathered numerous legends, magical beliefs and superstitions, such as lightning never strikes the elder, or that cutting it brings bad luck, possibly originating from the story that Judas Iscariot hanged himself from it.

The elder is tall and bushy, growing up to 10 m/32 ft. Some of the lower growth is often cut back to make a more manageable tree. Attractive garden varieties are the golden and the variegated. An American variety, *Sambucus canadensis*, has larger, more fragrant flowers, but is not always freely available.

Elder trees are deciduous. The leaves consist of leaflets with ragged-tooth edges that give off a distinct odour when crushed. A profusion of tiny, fragrant, lacy, creamy-white flowers in flat umbels appear in season and become bunches of small purple berries in the slightly cooler days of late summer to autumn.

Growing elder

Propagation is best done in spring from half-ripe wood cuttings or by the layering method (*see* p. 10). Generally the elder is not fussy about the soil it grows in, but won't do well under very dry conditions. It can be planted in the sun or semi-shade, but will flower best in the sun. Planted from seed, it should flower within three years.

Using elder

Cut branches of the elder hung near windows will discourage flies. The bark, leaves, flowers and berries are in fact all suitable for this purpose.

Just remember to chant the following charm when chopping off any part of the tree to protect yourself from harm:

❛*Awd girl give me of thy wood and I will give thee some of mine when I grow into a tree.*❜

Elderberry

A tea made with four teaspoons of fresh or two teaspoons of dried elderflowers to a cup of boiling water is a known comfort to those suffering from colds. And the same tea can also be used as a natural skin freshener.

Elder has wonderful culinary uses; the fresh flowers making an unusual pickle. To make this pickle, place two cups of flowers still on umbels in a glass jar. Bring one cup of cider vinegar to the boil and pour it over the flowers. Leave this for an hour, remove the flowers from the vinegar and drain. The flowers are now pickled and must be used immediately, say in a salad. Keep the flavoured vinegar to make salad dressing.

A delectable dessert can be made by soaking umbels of flowers in wine for a short time, dipping them in a light batter and then deep-frying them till golden brown. Dust the flowery fritters with castor sugar and serve with cream, but remember to remove the main stem first. Flowers can also be added to pastry or pancake, muffin, and bun mixtures.

To prepare the flowers, pick them early in the morning, wash them lightly and shake dry. Place them in a plastic bag and allow them to steam in the sun for a while. The tiny flowers can then easily be removed from the stems.

There are many old recipes for making elderflower wine and champagne – well worth a try if one can get enough flowers!

The rich purple berries, a good source of vitamins A, B, C, calcium, potassium and iron, are traditionally used to make jellies and jams. In Scandinavian countries a simple fruit soup is cooked up and served with dumplings. Berries can also be added to apple pie to liven it up and another idea that goes down well, especially with children, is to make a cough syrup from honey and berry juice. Never eat the berries uncooked though, they will play havoc with the toughest of stomachs!

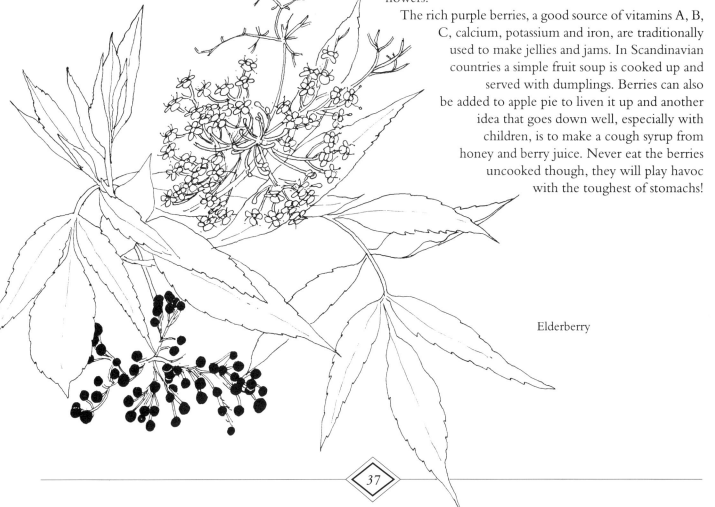

Elderberry

CALENDULA

Calendula officinalis

(Pot marigold)

Calendula has been grown in India since very early times where it is regarded as a sacred flower; wreaths of the flowers were used to garland statues of gods and godesses.

Calendula's botanical name refers to the plant's reputed habit of blooming on the kalends (the first) of every month. In rural England calendula is known as 'husbandman's dial' because the flowers open as the sun rises and continue to turn their faces to the sun as the day progresses, thus acting as a primitive clock. The Romans called it the herb of the sun. During the Middle Ages in England it was known as 'golds'. Its present name originates in the Anglo-Saxon *merse-mear-gealla*, meaning marsh marigold.

It hath pleasant, bright and shining
yellow flowers, the which do close at the setting downe
of the sunne, and do spread and open againe
at the sun rising.

Henry Francis Lyte

Growing calendula

Calendula is an annual, grown from seed sown in seed trays. You should sow in Autumn as calendula flowers throughout winter into early summer. Plant in full sun in an average soil – if your soil is too rich, the plants will produce leaves instead of flowers. It grows to a height of 30-50 cm/12-20 in.

Dwarf varieties that are suitable for containers are also available.

The foliage grows from stiff stems, producing bright green, oblong to oval leaves that are firm and slightly rough to the touch. The flat daisy-like flowers are orange to pale yellow, double or single, and some have very dark centres. The plants are prone to mildew which can easily be dealt with by a light application of vine dusting powder (flowers of sulphur).

Those who eat marigolds will see faeries, be more
amorous and be induced to sleep.

Anon.

Using calendula

Calendula petals are attractive and tasty when used with food, the flavour being slightly more sweet than salty.

Gerard advocates their use in stews, broths and to impart a rich flavour (and colour) to cheese. An old calendula pudding recipe is made of petals, sugar, lemon peel and juice, breadcrumbs and cream, and I often add petals to a simple steamed pudding for enhanced colour and flavour.

Pick the flowers before the sun is high, pluck the petals from the calyx and place them in the fridge until you need them. You might like to use them instead of saffron to give rice a yellow tinge. Parsley omelettes, salads, cheese

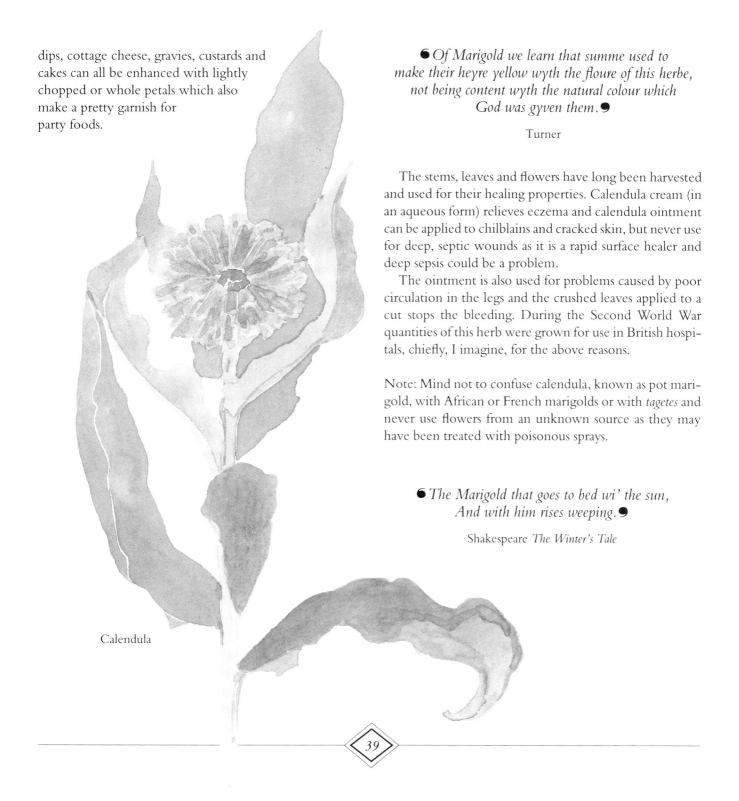

dips, cottage cheese, gravies, custards and cakes can all be enhanced with lightly chopped or whole petals which also make a pretty garnish for party foods.

Calendula

⚬ Of Marigold we learn that summe used to make their heyre yellow wyth the floure of this herbe, not being content wyth the natural colour which God was gyven them. ⚬

Turner

The stems, leaves and flowers have long been harvested and used for their healing properties. Calendula cream (in an aqueous form) relieves eczema and calendula ointment can be applied to chilblains and cracked skin, but never use for deep, septic wounds as it is a rapid surface healer and deep sepsis could be a problem.

The ointment is also used for problems caused by poor circulation in the legs and the crushed leaves applied to a cut stops the bleeding. During the Second World War quantities of this herb were grown for use in British hospitals, chiefly, I imagine, for the above reasons.

Note: Mind not to confuse calendula, known as pot marigold, with African or French marigolds or with *tagetes* and never use flowers from an unknown source as they may have been treated with poisonous sprays.

⚬ The Marigold that goes to bed wi' the sun, And with him rises weeping. ⚬

Shakespeare *The Winter's Tale*

SORREL

Rumex scutatus

(French sorrel, dock)

Sorrel is indigenous to Europe and North Africa and was introduced into Britain by the Romans. The Romans and Egyptians were known to use sorrel at their banquets to help counteract the effects of rich food and in Tudor times it was a most popular vegetable at the dinner table.

Growing sorrel

The tender-leafed sorrel is a perennial that loves to grow in rich soil in the sun or semi-shade. Should you however allow it to dry out in hot weather, it will soon droop. Increasing your sorrel stock can be done by dividing the roots or by sowing the seeds.

The oval, bright green leaves grow in clumps from a deeply rooted stem, the leaves having a characteristic arrow shape at the stem junction. They are succulent with brittle stems and have, as do the stems, a refreshing, sourish tang. But beware; snails enjoy a meal of sorrel so remove them at first sight.

Using sorrel

It is best to pick the leaves from the outside growth, as the young new shoots are vulnerable and the growth of the plant could be inhibited by their removal. Shredded leaves mixed into salads or a sauce for fish dishes add a wonderful touch, as will a cream of sorrel soup served as a starter. To make the leaves crisp, wash, dry and wrap them in paper toweling and keep in the refrigerator until needed. You could also cook sorrel as you would spinach or with spinach.

Sorrel has long been valued for its vitamin C content and use as an age-old treatment for scurvy. As there is a fair amount of oxalic acid present in the leaves, I don't recommend that people with acid-related problems, such as arthritis or gout, include sorrel in their diet.

In its natural state sorrel is found growing near stinging nettle, which is useful as it acts as an antidote to nettle rash.

Sorrel should not be confused with the long-stemmed, yellow-flowering *Oxalis pes caprae*, (Suring or Bermuda buttercup), which is a native of South Africa.

> ❧ *Sorrel sharpens the appetite, assuages heat, cools the liver and strengthens the heart; . . . together with salt, it gives both the name and the relish to sallets from the vapidity, which renders not plants and herbs only, but men themselves pleasant and agreeable.* ❧

Old herbal saying

PURSLANE

Portulaca oleracea

Purslane is native to India, Pakistan, southern Europe and Africa. Though it is seen as a weed in many warmer parts of the world, it has been part of man's diet for more than 1 000 years. Because of the herb's high iron and vitamin C content, thus preventing scurvy, it was popular with seafaring men who planted the seed in coastal areas frequented for victuals. Sailors introduced it to South Africa from the island of Ascension where it was referred to as the 'herb called porcelain'.

❦ *Lord, I confess too when I dine the pulse is thine —*
And all those other bits that be there placed by thee,
The worts, the purselain,
and the mess of Water Cress. ❧

Robert Herrick

Purslane

Growing purslane

Purslane is an easily-cultivated annual that could be grown from seed, if it does not already grow in your garden as a 'weed'. It is a sprawling plant, growing to 25 cm/10 in, producing a red-tinged stem as smooth and succulent as the red-rimmed, dark green leaves. There is a popular variety called *P. sativa* that has pale green leaves.

Sow the seed *in situ* as both kinds have long tap roots and do not transplant well. When the small yellow flowers appear the leaves are no longer worth eating. Purslane usually grows in hot, dry areas, and watered well, will produce even more succulent growth.

Using purslane

Always use purslane fresh as it is difficult to dry the thick, fleshy leaves. I strip the leaves and use them in mayonnaise for cold fish dishes and in mixed salads, as is done in certain parts of France. In the Middle East it is eaten raw in *fattoush* — a type of salad. The leaves are particularly tasty when pickled with fennel and used in salads.

Lightly chopped stems and leaves added to soups and stews in the last few minutes of cooking will provide added nourishment and flavour.

❦ *Purslayne is eminently cooling and generally entertained in all sallets.* ❧

15th century herbal

Nasturtium

Tropaeolum majus

Nasturtiums originated in Central and South America and were introduced into Europe by the Swedish botanist, Linnaeus. The generic name originates in an ancient custom: after battle, victorious armies would select a tree or set up a trophy pole known as the 'tropaeum' (trophy). On this they draped all the armour and equipment of the conquered as an emblem of victory. When Linnaeus discovered the trailing plant we know as nasturtium, he called it 'tropaeolum' because the round leaves with stems coming from the back looked like shields and the red and yellow flowers were reminiscent of blood-stained helmets.

Growing nasturtium

Modern varieties have double or single flowers, with or without spurs, and are compact in growth. They are best grown from seed sown directly into the ground as the plants prefer not to be moved. Perennial varieties will grow from cuttings (*see* p. 10).

For best results, sow the seeds in a sunny spot in well-drained soil. Lastly, and this has been done for many years, nasturtiums can be planted near a vegetable patch or under a fruit tree where they act as a pest deterrent and 'encourage fruitfulness'.

Using nasturtium

The flowers, buds, leaves and seeds are all edible. When used in salads and as garnishes, you will find the flowers have a milder, mustardy flavour whereas the leaves tend to be more peppery. Dried and powdered, the leaves can thus be used in place of pepper as a seasoning.

Make tasty canapés by stuffing the flowers with seasoned cottage cheese. Or pickle some green seeds in spiced vinegar and use as a substitute for capers. One or two seeds crushed in a salad dressing add piquancy and nasturtium flowers tossed in a salad or rice dish add a touch of colour. Don't overdo it with the nasturtiums though; this is a strong herb and needs to be used with care.

The leaves have antibiotic properties and chewing some will alleviate a sore throat. The juice from the plant dabbed onto facial pimples is known to clear them up.

An effective garden spray can be made from nasturtiums by crushing some of the plant material and adding to it some grated oil-based soap and covering it with boiling water. It can then be used to combat whitefly or aphids in the garden.

❝ *O vibrant hues of autumn gold*
speak of tales yet untold
embracing earth with twining arms
betraying all thy hidden charms ❞

Anon.

Nasturtium

BAY

Laurus nobilis

(Sweet bay)

This small tree, native to the shores of the Mediterranean, played an important part in Greek and Roman history. It was a symbol of honour and victory, worn by emperors and triumphant troops. Poets were awarded laurel wreaths, hence the title 'Poet Laureate'. The bay tree was formerly called the laurel, though the modern word bay comes from the French *baies*, meaning berries. Way back, students were crowned with wreathes of berried laurel branches, the 'bacca

Bay

lauris'. Upon completing a degree course today, we receive the *baccalaureate* degree and this degree in turn gave birth to the word 'bachelor' for an unmarried man, once a person too engrossed in studies to enter matrimony.

Generally speaking, the bay tree is said to have magical properties, protecting one from bad luck, lightning and illness. However, it also has evil undertones for death is predicted should a bay tree die.

Growing bay

The bay tree can grow up to 10 m/32 ft but will make a good container plant if kept clipped, either in standard or bush form. It will grow well indoors provided it is placed in a well-lit spot and the leaves are washed down periodically. The trunk has smooth, reddish-green bark and the branches and twigs bear dark green, ovate, leathery leaves. Some trees have slightly more elongated foliage. Small yellow flowers, which turn into hard green berries, before becoming deep purple berries, blossom at the base of the leaf stem.

The trees are sometimes attacked by sooty mildew and scale in which case an oleum spray will be needed, especially if the tree is large.

Neither witch nor devil, thunder nor lightning will hurt a man where a bay tree is.

Culpeper

Propagate from cuttings, layering (*see* p. 10) or from root suckers and plant the tree in full sun or semi-shade in hot areas. Good drainage is essential, as is regular watering. Occasionally hose down the plant to keep it free from dust.

❧ *Tis thought the king is dead; we will not stay. The bay trees in our country are all wither'd.* ☙

Shakespeare *Richard II*

Bay (leaf)

Using bay

The leaves have a strong spicy aroma, even more so when dried, and for many years have formed the basis of classic French cooking. Bay is also an essential herb in a bouquet garni and crushed leaves add a lovely, spicy smell to pot-pourri (*see* p. 14).

In olden times a small bundle of cooking herbs, including bay, was known as a 'Faggot of Herbs' and if they were tied in a small muslin square, a 'Dick Whittington'. Herbs were used in this way for easy removal before serving the food.

Bay leaves flavour milk puddings, casseroles, soups, stock and fish dishes and improve a marinade. I, for instance, use bay leaves together with lemon grass when boiling rice. Take care to use only mature leaves for cooking, and then with restraint, as the young ones have a higher acid content.

As the leaves contain traces of hydrocyanic acid, place them in bookcases and drawers to keep fishmoth (silverfish) at bay. And when storing pastas, rice, cereals or dried pulse vegetables, place a couple of leaves, dried or fresh, in the containers to prevent spoilage by weevils.

As for the berries, they have mild narcotic properties and their oil can be successfully applied to relieve rheumatism and heal bruises.

❧ *And when from Daphne's tree he plucks more Baies His shepherd pipe may chant more heavenly lays.* ☙

William Browne

LAVENDER

Lavandula spp.

Lavender supposedly got its name from the Latin *lavare* meaning 'to wash' which refers to its age-long use in bath-time oils and perfumes. It is native of the Mediterranean, used by Egyptians and Arabs domestically and cosmetically, and was brought to England during the 16th century where it immediately took to the soil. Though English lavender is the species most often used in the perfumery business – its scent being intensely aromatic – there are at least 28 other known species.

At one lavender farm in Norfolk (the home of the famous Mitcham lavender), they grow between 30 to 40 hybrids. And the royal estate at Sandringham produces a great deal of lavender for the flower and perfume trades.

Lavenders have been grown from time immemorial. Because it is so old, lavender is bound in folklore, tradition and superstition. Surprisingly the Romans, who brought

French lavender

many herbs to England, did not introduce this one, though some may beg to differ.

Lavenders are perennial shrubs varying in height, leaf formation and colour, flower colour and shape. Of all the varieties, the most easily obtained and grown are:

ENGLISH LAVENDER

Lavandula angustifolia

It has smooth, grey foliage with long spikes of lavender-coloured flowers. It grows to a height of 130 cm/50 in.

FINE FRENCH LAVENDER

Lavandula dentata

This lavender has serrated (dentate), green foliage with smaller flowers than var. *candicans* described below. It has a delicate, balsamic scent.

FRENCH LAVENDER

Lavandula dentata var. candicans

This lavender too has serrated foliage, though it is more grey in colour. The flowers are full, have cone-shaped heads and are also lavender-coloured. This variety generally has a good scent.

❧ *Comfort for the stomach and Braine.* ❧

Turner

Broad-leafed lavender

Lavandula latifolia

Also known as *ramosa*, this variety produces smooth grey foliage and sparse flowering — three spikes of dull mauve florets to a stem. It will attain a height of 150 cm/50 in and the foliage is highly scented.

Dwarf Hidcote and Munstead lavender

Cultivars of Lavandula angustifolia

These are low-growing varieties with compact, silver-grey foliage. Hidcote's flowers are almost blue and are loosely spaced on stems of about 15 cm/6 in. The Munstead's flowers appear as close three-pronged spikes on long stems.

Spanish or Italian lavender

Lavandula stoechas

This one offers fine, compact, grey-green foliage and flowers that are almost square, topped with a few purple wings. The flower stems are short, the plant attaining a height of 60 cm/24 in. The scent is not very strong.

If lavender grows well in the garden, the girls of the house will never marry.

Anon.

Growing lavender

Propagate all lavenders from heeled, ripe, new wood cuttings or by root division (*see* p. 10). In spring and autumn Spanish lavender will self-seed. Prune your lavender hard after flowering to keep the plant compact and to prevent woody growth. Keep in mind that lavender is an ideal plant for hedging.

A sunny, well-drained position is almost all that is needed, though the plants will enjoy the addition of a touch of lime to the soil.

Dwarf Hidcote lavender

English lavender

Using lavender

Lavender spikes retain their fragrance for a considerable time when dry, but must be harvested fairly early in the morning and then spread out to dry in an airy place in the sun. The Spanish used to extract oil from their lavender by hanging the lavender, flowers downwards, in a sealed wide-necked jar exposed to the sun. Though the oil is reputed to have stimulant and carminative properties, it is nowadays mainly employed in the making of perfumes, soaps and toiletries (*see* p. 17).

Both the leaves and flowers have a fresh, crisp smell and are used in medicines and in the perfume, cosmetic and toiletry industries. To make a lovely, natural lavender bath, steep two handfuls of dried lavender in two cups of boiling water and leave until lukewarm. Strain, add to the bath water and luxuriate.

Since the flavour is quite spicy, lavender should be used sparingly in food. It lends itself to mutton and chicken dishes and fish soup and a few chopped or separated flowers can be added to salads. In times past, cakes were iced with a blend of chopped flowers, rosewater and sugar – sounds delicious! Queen Elizabeth I was particularly fond of a lavender conserve served with meats.

For a calming and sleep-inducing tea, try mixing small though equal quantities of melissa, lemon verbena, peppermint and lavender flower heads and leaves into a cup of boiling water. Then pour a small quantity into a Thermos flask and drink if sleep eludes in 'the wee hours'. If that doesn't work, take a long, hot lavender bath and make yourself a pillow stuffed with, amongst other herbs, of course, lavender (*see* p. 15).

❦ *Lavender is of especial good use for all griefes and paines of the head and brain.* ❦

John Parkinson

Hortus Sanitatis suggested placing a sachet containing a collection of lavender flowers, bay leaves, rose petals, marjoram, cloves and nutmeg on the head as a cure for a bad headache — a harmless remedy worth trying.

The antiseptic qualities of this herb are useful in gargles and mouthwashes. A good handful of leaves simmered — not boiled — in two cups of water can then be left to cool and used as required.

Don't forget that the dried flowers and foliage are both essential to potpourri (*see* p. 14).

Treat a friend to some lavender soap that you can easily make yourself. Take 10 to 12 tablespoons of grated pure, unscented soap and place it in a bowl over a pot or pan of slowly boiling water. Stir the soap until it has melted. Make lavender oil by adding fresh lavender flowers to 300 ml/½ pint of slightly heated almond oil. Remove the flowers after 24 hours and add two tablespoons of the oil to the soap. Now mix in 2 tablespoons of clear honey and a few drops of blue or violet colouring. Pour your mixture into shaped, oiled moulds and leave until set.

❦Long alleys falling down to twilight grots,
Or opening upon level plots
Of crowned lilies, standing near
Purple-spiked lavender.❧

Tennyson

Dwarf Munstead lavender

CHAMOMILE

Anthemis nobilis

(Camomile, ground apple)

This lovely herb comes from southern Europe, temperate Africa and Asia, and was used by the ancient Egyptians as a cure for the plague. The pleasant apple aroma caused the Greeks to call it 'ground apple', derived from the words *chamai* (on the ground) and *melon* (apple).

It is used to flavour Spanish sherry known as Manzanilla, which means 'little apple'. The leaves consist of fine green threads and in summer slender stems shoot up from the plant, each bearing a white daisy-like flower with a brilliant yellow, raised centre.

In Britain, chamomile lawns have been prized since Elizabethan times, but in other parts of the world it will at most spread through the pathways.

Chamomile

Growing chamomile

Propagate your chamomile from runners during spring and keep the unused flowers cut down to foliage level. The annual or German chamomile, *Matricaria recutita*, will grow from seed to some 40 cm/16 in and has the same foliage, flowers and uses of the Roman variety. It is also sometimes known as scented mayweed.

Grow your chamomile in fertile soil in sun or semi-shade, never allow the shallow roots to dry out and keep the plant free from weeds.

Using chamomile

When using chamomile, it is best to use the dried flowers, so cut what you need with a pair of scissors on a clear day and spread out on racks or paper to dry.

A tea made from a dessertspoon of dried flowers and a cup of boiling water has an antiseptic as well as a calming effect. It is also known to improve the appetite and aid digestion. Try adding flowers to sour cream for baked potatoes, white sauce and herb butters and you'll be pleasantly surprised. It is also an excellent herb to use in sleep pillows and potpourri (*see* p. 14).

Like a chamomile bed —
The more it is trodden,
The more it will spread.

Spencer

FEVERFEW

Chrysanthemum parthenium

(Bride's button)

everfew is a perennial herb native to south-eastern Europe. It was listed among the 79 herbs taken up in the ordinance of AD 795, *Capitulare de Villis*, drawn up by Louis the Pious, son of Charlemagne, and was known as one of the herbs used to ward off the plague. It was named for its use in the treatment of fevers, but the showy, white flowers gave it a happier common name, 'bride's button'.

Feverfew might smell pleasant enough, but has a bitter taste. Its light green leaves have jagged edges. The plant consists of branching stalks that bear yellow-centred, white daisy-like flowers that are small and flat. Another variety of this species, known as 'white bonnets', has a double row of petals.

Growing feverfew

Feverfew will grow to a height of 45 cm/18 in if placed in a sunny spot – it tends to get mildew in shady places.

Propagate the doubled feverfew from heeled cuttings (*see* p. 10); the single feverfew will sow itself readily. It is a good idea to grow feverfew among plants prone to aphid attacks as it is the preferred host of these pests.

❦ *There're many feet on this moor tonight,*
And they fall so light as they turn and pass,
So light and true that they shake no dew,
From the featherfew and the hungry grass.❦

Nora Hopper *The Fairy Music*

Using feverfew

Feverfew must not to be taken from the garden by someone who does not know exactly what he or she is doing, as the true feverfew is difficult to identify correctly and mistakes are often made. Look out for feathery leaves. To this day feverfew is recommended for the treatment of migraine, rheumatism, arthritis and psoriasis.

Feverfew

NETTLE

Urtica dioica

The stinging nettle, native to the Mediterranean region, was spread by the Roman legions in their conquests all over central Europe and into England. The Roman soldiers planted nettles, which are rich in formic acid, in every country where they found the climate cold and because they could not stand the wet and chill of these regions, used to rub their limbs with the nettles to warm their blood. All I can say to this is that the sting resulting from the touch of a nettle leaf indeed causes a burning sensation, but whether it is pleasant probably depends on how cold it is!

In early Saxon writings nettle, known as 'wergulu', was regarded as a sacred herb and in medieval times the juice, pressed from the whole plant, was used as a medicine for tuberculosis. An infusion of the leaves served to relieve rheumatism and toothache.

Today nettle is a perennial herb (an annual variety does exist) found growing wild in many parts of the world.

Growing nettle

The perennial nettle can grow to 1 m/3 ft, especially in damp, rich soil and will grow in sun or dappled shade. The dark green, toothed, heart-shaped leaves coming to points, grow on stiff upright stems with small, greenish flowers, in catkin form, making an appearance in late summer. The plant is covered in fine hairs containing formic acid and this is what gives it its painful sting. Fortunately in the wild, an antidote in the form of sorrel usually grows nearby. Rub the affected part with sorrel leaves, plantain, bulbine, mint or the juice of nettle to relieve the burn.

Propagation should be from spreading root stock. You can plant nettles near ailing plants to stimulate their growth or near aphid-prone plants to keep this pest at bay.

Nettle

❛*They may be found, by feel, on the darkest night.*❜

Anon.

Using nettle

The Greeks believed that a flogging with branches of nettle dispelled bodily aches and pains. Maybe this is just a case of transferred pain? Nettle is to this day commonly used in hair remedies and shampoos, as it has been known since the Middle Ages to stimulate hair growth.

A few crushed stems of nettle placed in the middle of a compost heap (*see* p. 11) act as a magic activator. This is due to its potent chemical composition of mainly phosphate, nitrogen, protein, silica and iron. As far back as the 16th century farmers made a fertilizer from nettle by cutting the plant before it flowered and placing these cuttings in a wooden cask. It was then filled with rainwater and left to ferment for about a month. This mixture was used diluted with ten parts of rainwater and sprinkled on prepared soil. This recipe still works as a natural fertilizer today! Nettle can also be fed to poultry, as it is known to increase their egg-laying.

You can make nettle tea by adding half a cup of chopped leaves – use gloves to harvest – to two cups of boiling water. If you don't have any in your garden, dried leaves can be bought. Young tips are used to make nettle soup as they are rich in minerals (especially iron) and vitamins A and C.

Mind to only use the young tips for cooking, as the old growth tends to become gritty after developing silicic acid. Lightly fry young tips in butter or boil them in water and serve as a vegetable. Both the processes of drying and heating destroy the poison in nettle, making it quite safe to eat.

● *Nettle in, dock out*
Dock rub nettle out. ●

Old rhyme

Nettle

LEMON VERBENA

Lippia citriodora

Originally from South America where they call it *herba luisa*, this has been a well-loved and used plant in many parts of the world for centuries. It is a small, woody, deciduous shrub with lance-shaped, light green leaves which are slightly sticky to the touch and exude a strong lemon flavour and aroma. Plant it near a door or path so that in passing, the leaves can be brushed against and give off their scent.

It's a pity this lovely, strongly scented plant is so sensitive to cold weather, because to my mind it is a must in every herb garden.

Growing lemon verbena

It generally prefers a sunny position and as I said, does not do well in cold climates at all. Propagate the plant by taking soft cuttings in summer and hard cuttings in spring (*see* p. 10). When leaves are shed in winter, the plant should be pruned back hard to control the growth. Be sure to harvest a supply of leaves for use during the dormant period. The volatile oils are retained well when leaves are dried, making lemon verbena an important potpourri herb (*see* p. 14). If the weather is very hot and dry, I advise that you water the underside of the leaves to prevent an attack by redspider.

Lemon verbena

Using lemon verbena

Powdered dry leaves can be used as a salt substitute in a salt-free diet. If you are on a low salt diet, mix one teaspoon of sea salt with enough dried lemon verbena to taste and add dried crushed celery leaves for enhanced flavour.

I'm convinced lemon verbena was created for tea. Add a sprig of peppermint and you'll have a refreshing drink known as Egyptian Tea, also lovely served chilled. As a matter of fact, any mixed herb tea is improved with the addition of lemon verbena leaves and a tea made from fresh or dried leaves can safely be used as a sedative.

Another good idea with lemon verbena is to cook the leaves in milk puddings and custards. Or you can chop the young leaves and add them to cottage cheese, herb butter, white sauce for fish or egg sauce for veal. They will also improve the taste of fruit salads or pork and chicken dishes. Older leaves can be used whole in cooking, but take care to remove them before serving.

It grows along the old cathedral wall,
Where volcano shadows fall,
Herba Luisa of sweetest smell
Makes a tea as well.

A.G.S.

Lemon verbena

LEMON GRASS

Cymbopogon citratus

(Serai, sereh)

Native to south-east Asia, lemon grass is a true grass having long brownish green leaves which bend over softly. The leaves form a tubular sheath around the hollow stem coming from a bulb-like root known as a stolon.

Lemon grass is often used in the cooking of Thailand, the East Indies, Malaysia and other areas of south-east Asia where it is called *serai* or *sereh*.

Growing lemon grass

Propagate by removing the root-bearing stolons from the main plant and placing them firmly in rich moist soil – not too deep. Be patient, as the new shoots can take as long as six weeks to appear. Lemon grass will grow in full sun or semi-shade but needs sun-protection in very hot areas.

Using lemon grass

Lemon grass is commercially grown for the extraction of citronella oil, a well-known insect repellent. Also called lemon grass oil, it is used in cosmetics, detergents and soaps as well as for its antiseptic properties.

A tea made from a teaspoon of chopped leaves to a cup of boiling water makes a refreshing drink and is ideal for people who like lemon but cannot tolerate the acid. The tea is also useful in counteracting biliousness and of help to people with liver complaints. If any tea is left over, it makes a good rinse for oily or dull hair.

The pounded root and leaves are used in marinades, curries, soups, stews and rice, but remove the evidence before serving. The very young stems can be chopped for salads.

Lemon grass (root)

LEMON BALM

Melissa officinalis

(Bee balm, melissa)

Lemon balm grows naturally in the mountainous regions of southern Europe, though it originally came from the Middle East. The plant is slightly hairy and when bruised, the fragrant leaves attract bees in great numbers. Also known as melissa (Greek for bee), it is a sweet, lemon-scented perennial, growing in low clumps with short stiff stems producing light green crinkled leaves and small white flowers in season.

Growing lemon balm

Propagate in winter by dividing the plant into clumps. You may also find a few self-sown seedlings sprouting near the mature plant. But beware, small green caterpillars enjoy the leaves!

The lemon balm prefers semi-shade and a fair amount of water and it is a good idea to cut down the flowering tops from time to time to encourage fresh leaf growth. If rust appears, apply some copper spray, leave the plant unpicked for about a week and wash the leaves well before use.

Using lemon balm

This slightly antiseptic plant is well-known for its healing properties and crushed leaves can be applied to a wound.

A tea, made from fresh leaves and served with honey, has a calming effect and also helps 'to dispel melancholia'. It is reputed to clear the head, sharpen the understanding, improve the memory and to promote a long life.

On a culinary note, it adds zest when chopped and sprinkled on omelettes, salads, fish and rice. In Holland and Belgium the leaves are used to flavour pickled herrings and eels and the Spanish add lemon balm to their soups, sauces and milk dishes. I especially like the leaves in milk puddings.

The name 'bee balm' comes from apiarists' practice of rubbing the leaves on the inside of a new hive to encourage the swarm to stay.

*❧ Balm is sovereign for the brain,
strengthening the memory
and powerfully chasing away melancholy. ❧*

John Evelyn

*❧ The several chairs of order look you scour
With juice of balm and every precious flower. ❧*

Shakespeare

MINT

Mentha spp.

The name 'mint' is said to be taken from the Greek myth of the nymph Minthe, whom Pluto, the god of the Underworld, pursued with lust. This made his queen Persephone so jealous that she promptly turned the young nymph into a plant, our well-known mint, thereby doing away with the problem.

Mention is made in the New Testament of mint being used by the Pharisees to pay tithes and it is also known to be listed in the *Capitulare de Villis*.

A variety of mint can be found growing naturally in most parts of the world. It is a perennial herb with a creeping root stock and is characterized by a square stem and short, stalked leaves with whorls of small flowers in the axils of the upper leaves. Mint favours and thrives in damp, rich soil but because of its spreading nature it would be best to confine the plants. Watered regularly, mint will grow well and provide much joy in a container.

Growing mint

Propagation takes place from rooted pieces taken from a mature plant. You will find that mint is an easy-growing plant, but unfortunately some mints are subject to rust. If the problem is noted early, copper spray could stop this disease from spreading, but badly infected plants should rather be thrown out and replaced with new stock in a new position. As soon as the mint has flowered, cut the plant back to maintain a good supply of leaves. Some mints may die back during winter but they won't remain dormant for long. If you find your soil to be slightly acid, work in a small quantity of lime.

Mint

● *T'is said to 'Mendeth an ill savoured breath,' and 'stir up venery and bodily lust'.* ●

Anon.

58

English mint

Using mint

There are many ways of using the two most common varieties, which are spearmint *M. spicata* and round or English mint *M. rotundifolia*. Peas and new potatoes cooked with mint are simply delicious, or try chopped mint with honey and yoghurt as a cucumber dressing. Mint sauce and jelly are traditional accompaniments to roast lamb, and this reminds one of Pliny who wrote 'The smell of mint doth stir up the minde and taste to a greedy desire for meat'. Unknown to many, mint is also used in curries and offers welcome relief from an often overpowering flavour.

Mint, being a cool herb, is delicious used in ice cream and orange or lemon sorbet and the leaves frozen in ice cubes or a sprig of fresh mint dropped into your favourite cocktail makes for a refreshing drink. Mixed herb tea can be improved with the addition of mint and a simple mint tea served with a meal, will clear the palate and aid digestion. In the Middle East a heavily sugared mint tea is often served during the bargaining entailed in shopping. Remember that mint is a traditional and pretty garnish on a variety of dishes − sweet or savoury.

Commercially mint is used in toothpastes, gargles and chewing gum.

APPLEMINT

M. sauveolens

This is a variegated variety and its downy green, cream-edged to almost white leaves and small white flowers make an attractive border planting. Chop and scatter the sweetly scented leaves over a green or fruit salad or dry them for use in potpourri (*see* p. 14).

In the writings of Culpeper it is noted that applemint is 'a safe herb for biting of wild dog and good against venomous biting of serpents'. I would be somewhat hesitant about using mint like this, though.

Pennyroyal (flowering stem)

Pennyroyal (ground stem)

PENNYROYAL

Mentha pulegium

(Run-by-the-ground or lurk-in-the-ditch)

This is a low-growing plant, almost hugging the ground until summer when fluffy whorls of flowers appear on 25 cm/ 10 in long stems. These flowers will last well when cut.

Pennyroyal is often used as a ground cover between other plants as it acts as an insect repellent and a mulch, and a wonderful aroma will greet you when you walk on paving that pennyroyal has crept into. Pennyroyal is also sometimes known as 'fleabane' as it discourages fleas when rubbed into a dog's coat. Similarly it keeps mosquitoes at bay when rubbed on arms and legs. It will make a graceful plant in hanging baskets or pots.

Pennyroyal with its peppermint aroma is a strong herb and should only be taken internally under medical supervision. Externally 'it warms any part to which it is applied and digests corrupt matter', but it is also known to cause abortion in cattle – so don't plant it in your paddock!

Peppermint

PEPPERMINT

M. x piperita

This herb is recognized by its strong peppermint smell and taste and smooth green leaves on a slightly purple stem. The peppermint oil that we know so well is commercially distilled from the Japanese peppermint *M. arvensis*.

A sprig of peppermint with lemon verbena makes a pleasant, soothing herb tea which can be taken hot or chilled. When next making chocolate cake, first place some leaves in the bottom of the tin before pouring in the batter. One can also decorate cakes and desserts with crystallized peppermint leaves (*see* p. 16) or stir a few chopped leaves into a plain or chocolate ice cream mix before allowing it to set.

Peppermint is used in various medicines, cough mixtures and sweets. A stuffy head or blocked sinuses may be relieved by placing sprigs of peppermint in a small bowl and then covering them with boiling water. Place the bowl in a paper bag, hold the bag over your nose and mouth and inhale. The volatile oils given off will offer instant relief.

Spearmint

Watermint

WATERMINT

M. aquatica

(Fishmint)

If you have a pond or a boggy area in the garden this will be the ideal place to plant some watermint. It is a most decorative herb with tender, lime green leaves and long 30-90 cm/12-35 in spikes of lilac flowers. It is found in most temperate countries.

❛*There are as many kinds of mint as there are sparks flying from the mouth of a volcano.*❜

Anon.

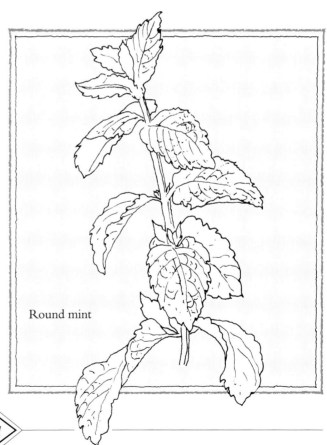

Round mint

ROSEMARY

Rosmarinus officinalis

(The dew of the sea)

Rosemary is a herb of many 'virtues' around which much myth and folk-lore has evolved; the Scandinavians believe that elves feast on the flowers and in Sicily the flowers are cradles for baby fairies. It was the custom at one time to grow rose-mary on graves in memory of loved ones and it was much in evidence at funerals, burnt as incense, and used in casting magic spells. Greek and Roman household gods wore wreaths made of rosemary, and students wove it into their hair to aid concentration and memory. Rose-mary has long been associated with the mind and improvement of the memory. Remember what Ophelia said in *Hamlet*: 'There's rose-mary, that's for remembrance', and similarly Culpeper agreed: 'It helps a weak memory and quickens the senses'.

Rosemary, native to Mediterranean coastal gardens, obtained its name from the Latin *ros* and *maris*, meaning 'dew from the sea' – this should hint as to where it grows easily . . .

Growing rosemary

An evergreen shrub growing to 90–150 cm/35–60 in, with a fresh, pungent smell reminiscent of resinous pine, rose-mary grows best in full sun in well-drained, alkaline soil. As the name 'dew from the sea' indicates, it does well at the coast, requiring protection in frosty areas.

The growth pattern varies, but with the exception of the rare 'gilded rosemary', the leaves are narrow, dark green on top and silver-grey underneath, growing densely on the branches. The flowers are single, their colour anything from white-rose to pale lavender and true blue. You might also find a double-white variety. Flowering time is inter-mittent from spring onwards.

O'Connell's blue rosemary

❛*Young men and maids do ready stand*
With sweet Rosemary in their hands –
A perfect token of your virgin's life.❜

Old ballad

Common rosemary   Creeping rosemary

❧ *The flowers rise in great numbers from the bosoms of the leaves, toward the upper part of the branches.* ☙

Culpeper

Common rosemary is upright in growth, a particularly good variety being 'Miss Jessup's Upright'. 'O'Connell's Blue' is one of the more spectacular blue flowering varieties but it needs space and the minimum of trimming. For pots, banks or garden walls, the small-leafed, creeping rosemary, *R. prostrata*, is both beautiful and functional.

Propagate from semi-hard cuttings taken during the growing season, which is autumn through winter, or by the layering method (*see* p. 10). Prune with discretion to maintain the shape and to promote growth on older wood. Rosemary will also make a successful hedge.

Using rosemary

As this is one of the strong herbs, it is advisable to chop and add to cooking with a light hand. Rosemary adds taste to milk puddings, scone, bread and biscuit batters, stews and of course, roasts. Flavour your apple jelly with rosemary to accompany roast pork or mutton and keep some rosemary vinegar on hand for salad dressing. The flowers are pretty and tasty added to salads.

On a non-culinary note, rosemary is a stimulating, invigorating herb when added to bath water or taken as a tea (one small sprig per cup). Steep a few larger sprigs in boiling water and when cold, you will find it an excellent rinse to make dark hair glossy. It is also said to prevent baldness when rubbed into the scalp.

Rosemary being strongly aromatic, is used commercially in eau-de-Cologne, toilet water, soap and shampoo. I use it in potpourri and sleep pillows because of its lovely, long-lasting aroma (*see* p. 14).

People used to say that rosemary had the power to make a person merry, happy and gay, to banish nightmares and to preserve youth. I am sure many of these benefits originated in the mind, because it is such a pleasant herb!

CRESS

Cruciferae spp.

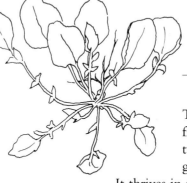

LANDCRESS

Barbarea verna

Landcress is a useful biennial taking the form of a low-growing rosette with a compound of lobed leaves, the outer, dark green leaves reaching out to 15 cm/6 in.

Growing landcress

Landcress self-sows readily and easily grows in sun or semi-shade, but the better the soil, the better the flavour. During their second year, bright yellow flowers appear which should be picked to ensure continued leaf production.

Using landcress

The pungent mustard-watercress flavour lends itself to salads, sandwiches, herbed cottage cheese mixtures and butters. Bear in mind not to use the leaves once flowering begins as they tend to become bitter.

WATERCRESS

Nasturtium officinale

The plant's generic name *nasturtium* comes from the Latin *nasi tortium*, meaning 'nose-twisting', in turn originating from its pungent taste and smell.

It thrives in soft-flowing streams — its sprawling stems rooted in mud, producing small, bright green leaves.

Growing watercress

Rooted pieces can be propagated in containers half-filled with wet soil. When the plants become established, keep the containers topped up with fresh water.

Using watercress

Always use fresh as drying destroys the flavour. It is good as a garnish or in salads, and makes excellent soup.

Watercress is a good overall tonic and fresh juice from the herb is said to clear the complexion.

CURLED CRESS

Lepidium sativum

Also called 'mustard and cress' as the seeds are sometimes sown in the same tray as mustard seeds.

This cress is excellent on egg sandwiches or in salads or omelettes. I have a childhood memory of mustard and cress growing in a dish of cottonwool on the kitchen windowsill . . .

Watercress

ROCKET

Eruca sativa

(Rocca or rocket-gentle)

ocket, a hardy plant from southern Europe, is sometimes also called American Rocket. It is an annual that sows itself, but to ensure a constant supply, I suggest you sow seeds throughout the year, especially as they are purported 'to make dour people merry'!

Growing rocket

Rocket is an easy-to-grow salad herb that produces leaves which are ready to pick within six to eight weeks of sowing. Upright in growth, rocket starts as a loose rosette and has dark green, indented leaves with purplish stems.

Rocket (flowers)

These leaves have a pleasant, nutty pungency, but are not nearly as biting as landcress. They appreciate full sun and a good rich soil and will even grow under poor conditions, but then the leaves tend to be tough and sometimes taste slightly bitter.

❧ *This Rocket Gentle, so called from the Italians, maketh one quicke and ready to jest and play.* ❧

John Parkinson

Using rocket

Rocket is a constant source of iron, sulphur, phosphorus and iodine as well as vitamins A and C. Scatter the leaves in salads or use them to make cheese sandwiches, but always use before flowering.

Culpeper advocates the making of a syrup with rocket for 'all stuffings of the breast and inveterate coughs' and though I haven't tried this I can vouch for 'good and wholesome for the stomach', as Gerard once said.

❧ *The seed bruised and mixed with a little vinegar, and of the gall of an oxe, cleanseth the face of freckles, spots and blew markes, that come by beatings, falls or otherwaies.* ❧

John Parkinson

SWEET VIOLET

Viola odorata

(Violet)

Violets have been grown and revered for thousands of years, and were the symbol of Athens as long ago as 1000 BC. In more modern times the violet was the emblem of the Imperial Napoleonic Party when Napoleon, known as Caporal Violette, was exiled to the island Elba.

Apart from various medicinal virtues, violets were also used as love charms and as a symbol of the Trinity in monastery gardens.

Violets are generally low-growing perennials with rooting runners coming from stolon-like roots. The foliage is dense, being deep green, heart-shaped leaves on slender yet firm upright stems. Beautiful perfumed flowers spring up between the stems. The most usual colour is purple, but there are also mauve, pink, white, variegated and double-flowered varieties. The lovely perfume of violets, for which they are in fact widely cultivated, has been likened to that of sun-ripened apricots.

Growing sweet violets

One would best propagate violets from rooted runners. This should be done during a cool spell in spring, as these plants flower during winter in most areas. Soil, well-composted with rotted manure, and a fair amount of sunshine will do just fine.

I find that too much shade and artificial fertilizers produce a mass of leaves to the detriment of flowers. If the growth is too dense, cut out some leaves; this will give the flowers a new lease of life. Also divide the clumps when they become too compact.

Violets

❛ *That which above all yeilds the sweetest smell in the air is the violet.* ❜

Sir Francis Bacon

Using sweet violets

The Romans added flowers to wine as it was said to prevent 'dizziness produced by taking too much wine'. Violets were also used as a substitute for honey to sweeten various Roman and Greek dishes.

A few fresh flowers added to light soups and chicken dishes in the last five minutes of cooking will produce an unusually pleasant flavour, and the flowers can also be used to decorate desserts or tossed into salads. If you have a jar of indifferent honey, add a few flowers to improve the flavour.

Crystallized violets (*see* p. 16) have long been used as sweetmeats and prettily decorate cakes and cookies. And if you have any flowers left after this, add them to your pot-pourri for colour and scent.

On a medicinal note, the leaves, having antiseptic properties, were used to make solutions to wash wounds and sores. An old herbal suggests that nursing mothers suffering from cracked nipples apply a poultice of bruised violet leaves to lessen the discomfort and traditionally the Greeks used violets to induce sleep and cure headaches; as someone said: 'the flowers do mollify'.

As a calmative and cure for most headaches, I suggest you drink a tea made from four leaves and five flowers to a cup of boiling water. If suffering from postnasal drip, try drinking this tea an hour before bedtime and again first thing in the morning.

❧Reform the errours of the Spring;
Make that the tulips may have share
Of sweetness, seeing they are fair;
And Roses of their Thorns disarm;
But most procure
That Violets may a longer Age endure.❧

Andrew Marvell

❧Annoint thy face with goat's milk in which violets have been infused, and there is not a prince of earth who will not be charmed with thy beauty.❧

Old Celtic saying

You can make delicious violet syrup that is not only a gentle laxative but is also helpful for coughs and bronchitis and soothes tired nerves. Simply place about six handfuls of fresh flowers in a cup of boiling water. Cover and leave to infuse for 24 hours. Carefully strain through muslin or cheesecloth, making sure you get all the liquid out of the flowers. Pour the liquid into a pan and add eight heaped tablespoons of honey. Slowly heat the mixture, and gently stir until the honey is dissolved. Remove the pan from the heat just before the syrup boils. Cool, bottle and store in a cool place.

Violets

TANSY

Tansy was first recorded in Charlemagne's list of herbs in AD 812. During medieval times in Britain tansy puddings or cakes were traditionally eaten on Easter Sunday to celebrate the end of Lent and in Elizabethan times it was used as a culinary and medicinal herb, but since even the smallest quantity has been found to be highly toxic, it is no longer used in cookery and medicinally only in doses correctly prepared by qualified people.

A classical legend has it that a drink made from tansy was given to a beautiful young man named Ganymede, Zeus's cup bearer, in the hope that it would make him immortal.

Tansy (flower)

Growing tansy

A perennial growing up to 1 m/3 ft before dying back in winter, tansy grows best in rich, moist soil, but will survive under less favourable conditions. Though tansy can be planted in either full sun or semi-shade, curly tansy must be kept away from the burning midday sun. Tansy has dark green feathery leaves from which erect stems of flat-topped clusters of yellow flowers appear in summer and autumn.

Gerard describes tansy as 'a plume of feathers', a very apt description. Curly tansy *T. crispum* is an attractive, lime green plant which rarely flowers and has a more compact leaf formation which tends to curl down.

Propagation is best from roots or cuttings (*see* p. 10). Curly tansy is less likely to spread than tansy and does not form such a tight mass; lifting and thinning is advisable when clumps become dense. Watch out for snails and slugs which lurk in these plants.

The name 'tansy' is derived from the Greek *athanato* which means immortal, and tansy was given this name because its flowers are so long-lasting.

❝ *On Easter Sunday be the pudding seen*
To which the Tansy lends her sober green. ❞

The Oxford Sausage

68

Using tansy

Because tansy is potentially toxic, I do not recommend using it in food, and pregnant women should avoid it at all cost. It was, however, used in the past to flavour sausage, omelettes, stuffings, to preserve meat and as a colouring agent or dye.

Because of its fernlike foliage and clusters of buttonlike, bright yellow flowers, tansy makes an attractive addition to the perennial flower garden.

Tansy should be harvested at ground level just before the flowers have fully opened. Hang the stems upside down and dry them in a dark, dry, airy place.

The distinctly sweet, spicy, lemon scent has made tansy a popular strewing herb. It can be bruised, dried or infused and strewn on doorsteps to keep ants and mice away. The plants grown around the outside of the house will discourage a variety of insects from entering. It is also a pleasant addition to anti-moth mixtures and can be used on its own in cupboards and drawers to deter fishmoths. Because of these properties, fresh leaves rubbed into a dog's coat will also help keep fleas away.

The spicy lemon scent as well as tansy's antiseptic properties, was why this potent plant was used by the Egyptians as an embalming herb. They rubbed it on corpses 'to prevent them from corruption'.

The strong perfume from dried flowers and foliage makes it an ideal ingredient in potpourri (*see* p. 14) and sachets, and as the dried flowers retain their colour well, they make lovely dried arrangements. You could also boil the flowers for a natural, golden yellow dye, and the leaves and stems for a yellow-green dye.

Tansy has a soothing, sleep-inducing effect, so use it in your bedtime bath or in a sleep pillow (*see* p. 15). Infused tansy can be used as a wash for bruises and sprains, but use with caution on sensitive skins.

Lastly, because of its potassium content tansy is also an important compost activator (*see* p. 11).

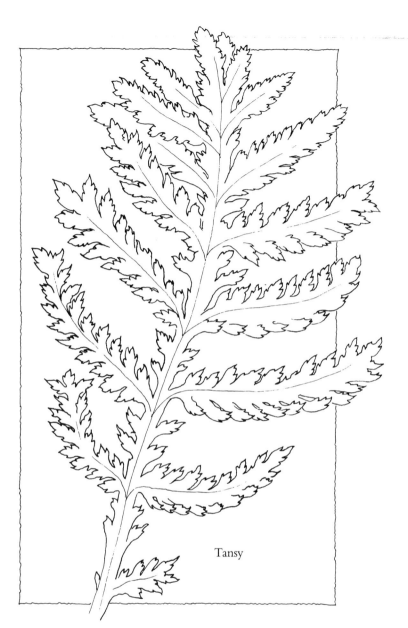

Tansy

❦ *Some camomile doth not amiss with savory and some tansy.* ❦

The Muses' Elysium

THYME

Thymus vulgarus

Thyme was originally found in countries bordering the Mediterranean and it was the Greeks who originally named this herb, taking it from the word *thymos*, meaning strong and manly. There are variant meanings, though, which are to fumigate or to sacrifice, referring to the use of its fragrant, balsamic wood as incense-bearing firewood in temples. The Egyptians also often used it as one of their embalming herbs.

Thymol, the oil in common thyme, and cymol, the oil in wild creeping thyme, are highly perfumed and effective antiseptics. Bees are greatly attracted to the flowers, and the delicious honey, reputed to be of the finest flavour and quality,

Variegated
lemon thyme

has been collected from Mount Hymettus in Greece since ancient times.

In the days of chivalry, thyme, like borage, was considered a symbol of courage, and sprigs of thyme on which a bee was perched were embroidered on crusaders' garments. It became a symbol of courage in medieval times when thyme was used in drinks and cordials, the slightly intoxicating properties giving men courage and bravado.

Thyme was also known as the symbol of the Republicans in France, and whenever a secret meeting was called, a sprig of thyme was sent to the members' houses.

The many varieties of thyme would fill a book on their own. I once saw 27 varieties on one herb farm in England and apparently this was only half of them! Common thyme is well known — it is a small, evergreen perennial shrub growing to 30 cm/12 in in temperate climates. The roots are fibrous and woody, while the twiggy branches are loosely covered with pairs of small, firm, dusky, grey-green leaves, which give off a warm aromatic taste and smell.

Lemon thyme, *T. citriodorus*, with dark green, gold or silver-grey foliage and pink flowers, is another kind grown widely for perfume and flavour. It is a low-growing plant with softer, rounder leaves growing denser on the stalks.

All thymes flower in pretty whorls on stem tips. The low-growing and creeping varieties make a lovely soft, colourful carpet. Depending on the plant, the flower colours range from white, pink and mauve to the deep purple of the miniature alpine thyme.

Growing thyme

Propagate your thyme from layering, cuttings, root division or from seed (*see* p. 10). All thyme grows well in a sunny position in well-drained soil. The low-growing and creeping varieties are best used for borders and are ideal for growing, to name but one place, between paving slabs in pathways. Trim the plant from time to time and keep in mind that thyme can be grown in containers for patio gardens or sunny windowsills.

In old English gardens, small hillocks of thyme were grown for, as was once believed, fairies to play or sit on.

> ❛*Luxuries of luxuries! I've been lying on my own thyme lawn, there was just enough room to turn over without landing on to the surrounding rock plants. You haven't lived if you have not lain flat on your middle on a thyme lawn.*❜

Edna Walling

Using thyme

Culpeper says: 'It is so harmless you need not fear for use of it' and common and lemon thyme are the ones most often used, their sprigs being some of the herbs used to make bouquet garni.

Harvest the branches just before the plant flowers and hang up in a shady place for two or three weeks. Strip or rub the leaves from the stalks and store in airtight glass jars until used to flavour cottage cheese, sausages, rissoles, meat loaf, fish salads, fishcakes, marinades, vinegar and oil (*see* p. 16) and so on, but use sparingly for it is strong-flavoured.

Lemon thyme is particularly useful when a hint of lemon is needed and the purists may object, but I find thyme leaves very good in Yorkshire pudding batter.

In Arab kitchens a sauce known as Za'-atar is made by mixing together thyme, sesame seeds, salt, coriander and

Lemon thyme

Common thyme

Greek thyme

oil. To make thyme vinegar, crush a small handful of leaves in a mortar while heating two cups of white wine vinegar to just below boiling point. Pour this over the leaves in an air-tight container, seal and leave to stand in a dark place for two to three weeks. Then strain through muslin into a serving bottle, add a fresh sprig of thyme and cork the bottle. This vinegar is excellent for salads, sauces and marinades, but is also known to ward off insects, to treat bites and, believe it or not, as a suntan lotion.

The Romans drank a thyme brew to lift depression and Culpeper treats 'headache occasioned by the debauch of the preceding night', meaning that it might cure a hangover. If you want to try this, or maybe just relieve a nagging cough or chest cold, mix one tablespoon of fresh leaves with a cup of boiling water and enjoy any time of the day.

Thyme also has useful antiseptic properties for a gargle or mouthwash and is used as a flavour and perfume in toothpastes, soaps, deodorants and hair lotions. I often enjoy a refreshing thyme herb bath.

❧ *For he painted the things that matter,*
The tints that we all pass by,
Like the little blue wreaths of incense
The wild thyme breathes to the sky. ❧

Alfred Noyes

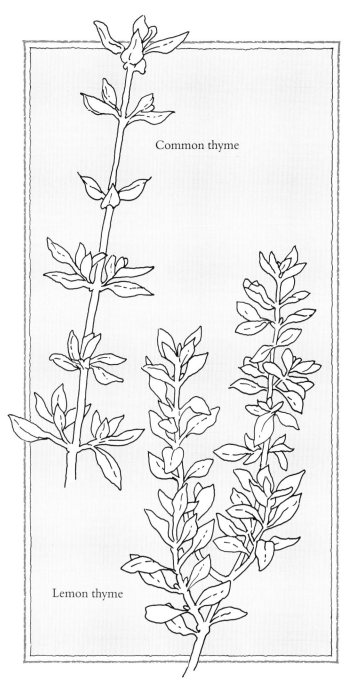

Common thyme

Lemon thyme

YARROW

Achillea millefolium

(Woundwort, Carpenter's weed)

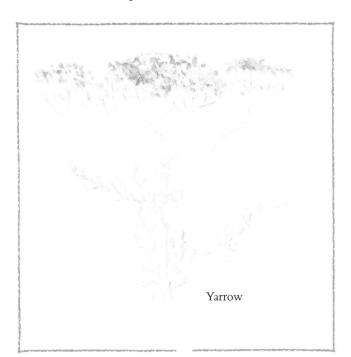

Yarrow is one of the oldest known plants in the world, fossilized yarrow pollen having been discovered dating back to Neanderthal times. Also, the Chinese used it some 4 000 years ago. Its generic name *Achillea* is derived from the story that Achilles reportedly used it to bind up his soldiers' wounds during the Trojan War. It is also known by names such as Woundwort and Carpenter's weed.

Yarrow

Growing yarrow

It is an attractive plant to grow in the full sun. Clumps of feathery leaves about 15 cm/ 6 in tall are brought forth with colouring varying from dusty grey to bright green, depending on the variety. In summer stalks shoot up to 60 cm/24 in and produce flat white umbels of small, closely packed flowers. The original flowers were white, pinkish or lilac, but attractive cultivars have been developed which have deep red, yellow, cream, rose or apricot flowers. The flowers dry well if they are hung upside down when mature but still bright.

Plants can by raised from root division as the plants tend to spread rapidly, but replant the clumps in a good quality soil every two to three years. Surplus plants are a welcome addition to the compost heap as they have wonderful activating properties (*see* p. 11). If spare plants are not available when you start making compost, you can chop up handfuls of leaves. It is also a good idea to plant a clump near ailing plants, as yarrow seems to strengthen the growth of other plants whilst also enhancing their fragrance.

❦ Yarrow which grows in a church yard is a reproach to the dead, who need never have come there, had they taken their Yarrow broth faithfully everyday while living. ❧

John Gerard

Using yarrow

As yarrow is a gentle herb it can safely be used in home remedies; the ability of this herb to stanch bleeding and its healing qualities are still made use of to this day. When working in the kitchen or garden, try it for those annoying cuts which seem to bleed forever.

As a gargle for a sore throat add a good handful of leaves to 1 ℓ/35 fl oz of boiling water, steep until cold, strain and use as required. The same mixture rubbed gently into the scalp is said to prevent balding. For a blood purifier and diuretic, take a heaped tablespoon of chopped leaves to a cup of boiling water and add a little lemon and honey to make it more palatable. Sipped warm it will also reduce feverishness associated with colds and flu.

Yarrow is sometimes known as the 'Venus tree' and used in bridal bouquets to ensure seven years of love.

Yarrow makes an excellent face pack for oily skins that tend to break out. Place some washed and finely chopped fresh leaves and flowering tops and a few drops of lemon juice in a pan with sufficient water to prevent burning. Bring to the boil and simmer for 10 minutes until a thick pulp is formed. Spread this onto a piece of muslin and put onto the face while still warm. Avoid eyes and mouth. Leave on for 10 to 15 minutes, then rinse off with luke-warm water.

Yarrow

Thou pretty herb of Venus tree
Thy true name it is Yarrow
Now who my bosom friend must be,
Pray tell thou me to-morrow.

J. O. Halliwell

CELERY

Apium graveolens
(Smallage, wild celery)

Celery originally came from the coastal areas of the south-eastern Mediterranean and to this day in the wild mostly grows in salty soil. The Greeks and Romans regarded it as a symbol of grief, eating it at funeral banquets and placing wreaths on graves. Many say it was the potherb originally known as smallage, or wild celery. It reached England sometime during the reign of Queen Elizabeth I when it was used both medicinally and in food.

Celery

Growing celery

Celery is grown from seed sown in spring or autumn and is a biennial in most areas. It will do well in the full sun planted in well-composted soil and kept moist. If you prefer blanched celery stalks, heap the soil around the plant as it grows or cover it with a cloche.

Your celery should produce a head of almost white flowers in the summer of its second year.

Using celery

The strongly aromatic seeds are mostly grown in France, India and America. The seeds, also used in pickles and stuffing, are dried, ground and mixed with refined salt to make delicious celery salt. The seeds can also be ground and mixed with dried lemon verbena to make a wonderful seasoning for a salt-free diet. The stalk, though, is the most commonly used part, serving both as a salad and as a vegetable. The peppery leaves in turn are excellent added to soups and stews. In ancient times the roots and stems were brewed as a remedy for upset stomachs and celery is still used as a nerve tonic and sedative.

❛I'm afraid of losing my obscurity.
Genuineness only thrives in the dark.
Like celery.❜

Aldous Huxley

LOVAGE

Levisticum officinale

(Maggi)

A somewhat neglected herb that was popular in ancient Greece and Rome, lovage is a native of the Balkan countries. In later years it was a favourite in colonial gardens and greatly esteemed for use in salads, soups and for scenting baths. It is described by Culpeper as having 'long green stems with winged leaves divided into many parts, being of a sad green colour'. It is also known as maggi since it was used as an ingredient in the popular Maggi products still known today.

It is a herb of the Sun, under the sign Taurus. It opens, cures and digests humours, and provokes womens' courses and urine.

Culpeper

Growing lovage

The perennial lovage grows best in a cool, moist, semi-shade position. As it can almost disappear in winter, I suggest you mark the area where you planted it in case you accidentally disturb the roots.

Lovage

Lovage self-seeds readily. Feed your lovage with well-rotted manure as soon as you spot new growth. Be on the lookout for snails, though, they love lovage.

Propagate from root stock and seed sown in trays in early spring.

Using lovage

Resembling celery in appearance, odour and taste, it can be used in much the same way. The seeds can be used sparingly to flavour rice, tomato and pasta dishes and the young leaves chopped and added to soups, stews, salads and white sauces. The seeds can also be coated with sugar or the stems candied and used in confectionery as a substitute for angelica. The leaves dry well and can be stored for winter, but remember what Culpeper said: 'Every part of it smelleth strongly and aromatically and hath a hot, sharpe, biting taste', so use it with thought. It also made a popular cordial in its time, taken to relieve sore throats and quinsy. Lastly, a refreshing bath can be made by tying fresh leaves in a muslin cloth and placing it in the flow from the hot water tap. Try it and enjoy a lovely bath.

PARSLEY

Petroselinum crispum

(Curled parsley)

Parsley is native to the Mediterranean region where it was used by the Greeks as a symbol of fame and joy and to garland heroes. It was also used for funeral rites, thus giving rise to much superstition regarding the sowing, planting and transplanting of parsley. Parsley, one of the first plants used in making wreaths, was first recorded as a culinary herb when Charlemagne compiled his herb list. It only reached England in the 16th century and was one of the herbs taken to America by the first British settlers.

Flat or Italian parsley, *P. c.* 'Neapolitanum' has flat fern-like leaves and grows taller than the curly variety. The flavour of the leaves is more pronounced and the plant does not go to seed in hot weather as readily as do other varieties.

Growing parsley

The curly leaves of *P. c.* 'Crispum' make it an attractive border plant for the herb or flower garden. This variety is the best kind to grow in a trough or pot which must be as deep as the roots are long. The foliage grows to about 20 cm/8 in.

Parsley is a biennial grown from seed. To keep a constant supply, sow at regular intervals. Seed takes up to three weeks to germinate, provided the soil is kept moist during this time. After going to seed, the plant dies.

Grow in the sun in the garden and if grown indoors, on a sunny windowsill.

Using parsley

Leaves are picked from the outer growth of the plant and occasionally the centre ones may be nipped out. Chopped parsley enhances savoury dishes, cottage cheese, and herb butters. Do not cook the leaves but chop them and sprinkle on or stir into food before serving. The high chlorophyll content helps to sweeten the breath, especially after eating garlic.

Hamburg parsley, *P. c.* 'Tuberosum' has similar foliage to flat parsley, but is grown mainly for its root, which has a

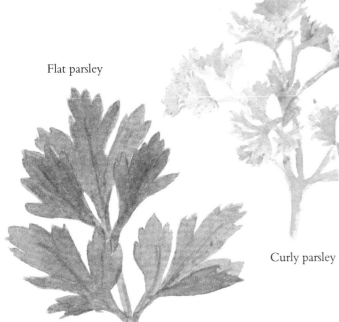

Flat parsley

Curly parsley

flavour reminiscent of celery and parsnip. Cook it just like you would parsnip or add to soups and stews.

Because parsley is rich in calcium, iron and vitamins A, B₁, B₂ and C, it should be included in our every-day diet, especially as we grow older. It is a natural diuretic, helping to clear the body of uric acid and has been advocated for reducing high blood pressure.

It is said that if a quantity of parsley is eaten daily, one's skin gives off a very seductive scent — better than any per-fume. Be warned.

Parsley (flowers)

At Sparta's Palace, twenty beauteous mayds,
The pride of Greece, fresh garlands crowned their heads
With hyacinths and twining parsley drest,
Grased joyful Menelaus' marriage feast.

Theocritus

SOUTHERNWOOD

Artemisia abrotanum

(Old man, lad's love, maiden's ruin)

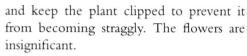

The name Southernwood is a corruption of southernwormwood and was first mentioned in the writings of a Benedictine monk, Walahfrid Strabo, in AD 840.

In the olden days young men rubbed their faces with southernwood to promote beard growth and gave nosegays, containing the herb, to the maidens of their choice as love tokens – hence the old names. The plant has a sweet, penetrating smell due to the presence of the oil absinol.

Growing southernwood

This herb is a woody perennial sub-shrub with feathery, grey-green leaves, growing to about 60 cm/24 in in height. Plant it in full sun or semi-shade in well-drained soil and keep the plant clipped to prevent it from becoming straggly. The flowers are insignificant.

Propagate by layering or by half-stripped cuttings, each about 15 cm/6 in in length (*see* p. 10).

Using southernwood

In Elizabethan times an extract of the oil contained in southernwood was used as a vermifuge. Today it is rarely used medicinally, and then only under medical supervision.

The perfume being long lasting, southernwood was a popular strewing herb and today an excellent addition to potpourri (*see* p. 14) or herb bags. As the French name 'garderobe' implies, it is an excellent moth-repellent.

Other uses include rubbing the head with a solution made from two tablespoons of chopped southernwood in one and a half cups of boiling water – this just might clear up any dandruff problems.

> ❦ *Admire too the tall bushes of southernwood*
> *with their bloom of down,*
> *and the sharp spikes which grow on its wealth of*
> *branches like finest hair.*
> *It is good to mix the scented sprigs, plucked with the*
> *supple stem, into healing medicines.* ❦
>
> Walahfrid Strabo

Southernwood

Nosegay with
Southernwood
border

*The ashes mingled with old salad oil,
helps those that are bald, causing the hair to grow
again on the head or beard.*

Anon.

SAGE

Salvia officinalis

(Common sage)

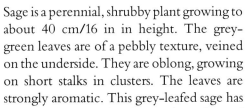

The generic name *Salvia* comes from the Latin word *salvere* which means to be in good health, to cure and to save.

Common sage is a Mediterranean herb, the most flavoursome being found in Yugoslavia. It is mentioned as far back as AD 812 in Charlemagne's list of herbs and for centuries was praised for its healing properties and ability to increase life span. As the old Arab saying goes: 'Why should a man die whilst sage grows in his garden?'

It is also used to flavour food and the Romans and Greeks often added sage to their food to make the rich dishes more digestible.

Sage is a perennial, shrubby plant growing to about 40 cm/16 in in height. The grey-green leaves are of a pebbly texture, veined on the underside. They are oblong, growing on short stalks in clusters. The leaves are strongly aromatic. This grey-leafed sage has spikes of pink or purple flowers. The plum-coloured or red sage is most commonly used medicinally. Then there is the golden-leafed variety and the lovely tricolour, with its leaves splashed with pink, green and cream. The last three forms rarely flower.

Growing sage

Propagation is from cuttings, seed or by root division (*see* p. 10). Sage grows best in full sun in well-drained, composted alkaline soil and will grow quite successfully in a large container. Remember to keep a continuous supply of rooted cuttings as sage has a disconcerting habit of suddenly dying off. Also keep a watch out for pests and cut out the dead wood and old flower heads from time to time to give new growth a chance.

Using sage

For cooking, sage is best harvested before flowering. Include it in the preparation of rich meats, poultry, sausage and oily fish or serve an apple-based sage jelly with pork, duck or goose. Add some to your next cheese omelette, pancake or fritter batter, and try to find that delicious sage cheese at your delicatessen.

Plum-coloured sage

Pineapple sage

In Switzerland, the leaves are sometimes dipped in batter and fried and because of the resulting shape, are called mice. And in Holland, during winter, a warm, sage-flavoured milk is a favourite on coming in out of the cold. Some people even sprinkle chopped sage on porridge – enough to upset a good Scot! This is a strong herb, though, so use with a light hand.

To darken grey hair, simmer 1 *ℓ*/35 fl oz of dried sage to four tablespoons of used tea leaves in one litre of water for 15-20 minutes. Strain and rub the solution into your hair every day for a week, then weekly. For a gargle or mouthwash for ulcers, steep about two tablespoons of fresh leaves in one cup of hot vinegar, then add a cup of cold water. Strain and refrigerate.

A tea made with four to five leaves, sipped warm, helps clear phlegm and stops a nagging cough and leaves can be chewed to whiten teeth and sweeten the breath. Sage has strong antiseptic properties which also act as a deodorant when used in a bath.

PINEAPPLE SAGE

Salvia rutilans

An attractive, perennial Mexican plant to grow in the flower or herb garden. Pineapple sage has firm, red-tinged stems, from which strong, soft, hairy, light-green leaves grow. Spikes of bright red flowers appear in autumn and winter and being heavy with nectar, present a great attraction to bees and small birds.

Growing pineapple sage

Increase your stock by propagating from cuttings (*see* p. 10) or sucker roots. Sage prefers full sun but I have grown it in dappled shade where it does not flower as well. Plant it in well-drained, lightly-composted soil and watch out for damage from frost. Cut your plant down to its base after flowering and thin the clumps out from time to time.

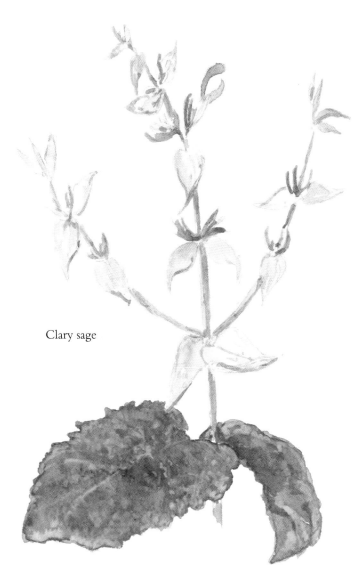

He that would live for aye, must eat Sage in May.

American folk saying.

Clary sage

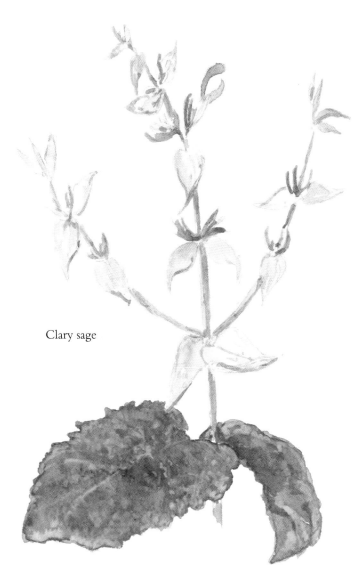

Using pineapple sage

The leaves and flowers have a pronounced pineapple scent and flavour and, lightly chopped, do wonders for green or fruit salads. When adding the chopped leaves to pork or chicken dishes, do so at the end of the cooking time so as not to lose the flavour. Pineapple sage leaves on their own or mixed with other herbs, make a refreshing tea that can be served hot or chilled. Add dried leaves to potpourri mixtures (*see* p. 14) for pineapple fragrance.

CLARY SAGE

Salvia sclarea

A southern European relative of common sage with, to quote Culpeper, 'a sweet strong scent'. I have found that when the flowers are mature, their smell is actually decidedly unpleasant.

Growing clary sage

Clary sage is supposed to be biennial, but I treat it as an annual which seeds itself. The seed can be sown in well-manured soil in a sunny position from late winter onwards, conditions not being too severe. Clary sage generally is a large plant with soft, furry grey-green wrinkled leaves, and spectacular spikes of orchid-like bracts supporting its small flowers.

The flowers and bracts can be cream, pink, lilac, white or mauve in colour and should be cut back once the seeds have been collected.

Sage is singularly good for the head and the brain;
it quickeneth the senses and the memory; strengthen the
sinew; restoreth health to those that hath the palsy;
and takes away shaky trembling of the members.

John Gerard

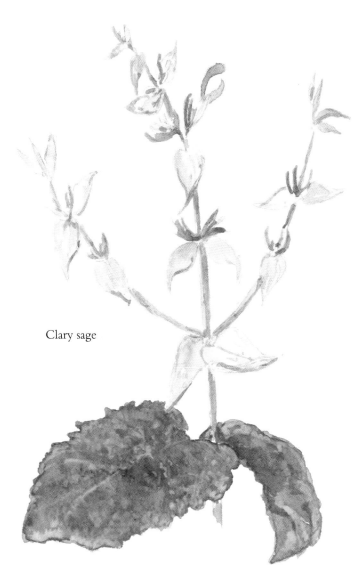

Using clary sage

The seeds, when crushed, give off a fruity scent and act as a fixative when added to potpourri. Grown commercially, the lavender-like oil is greatly valued in the perfume industry and was once used to make clary wine which was considered an aphrodisiac.

Culpeper says, 'its name is more properly Clear Eye' and a somewhat drastic method of clearing eyes of foreign bodies, taken from an old herbal, reads: 'Boil water and soak a few clary seeds in it. Leave seeds until mucilaginous – introduce into corner of eye – foreign bodies will stick to mucilage and can be removed with seed'. I definitely don't recommend this procedure!

An ointment or compress made with clary leaves will, however, help to draw out inflammation quite safely and will bring boils and spots to a head. To make clary ointment, fill a saucepan with crushed fresh leaves and cover with vinegar. Cover the pan and simmer over low heat for one hour. Strain off the liquid, discard the leaves and repeat the process with fresh, crushed leaves. After this second lot has simmered for a further hour, allow to cool and press all the vinegar out of the leaves. Add sufficient honey to the vinegar to make a soft ointment.

To make a compress, steep 50 g/2 oz of dried clary leaves in 600 ml/6 oz of vinegar for two weeks and apply.

❡Marbled with Sage the hardening cheese she pressed.❡

Gay

Tricolour sage

Cotton Lavender

Santolina

(Lavender cotton, Santolina)

Cotton lavender, native of southern Europe and North Africa, is one of the most ornamental herbs. It has a strong odour and is a member of the daisy family, and not of the lavender family as many may think.

Growing cotton lavender

Santolina does best planted in full sun in dry or moist, but perfectly drained soil – thus making it an ideal plant for coastal gardens.

Cotton lavender (flower)

Keep all the varieties well-clipped, removing the flowers as they die to keep the plants neat and to allow them to bush out with new growth. The attractive yellow flowers will last well in water and also dry successfully.

Propagate by layering and cuttings in sand (*see* p. 10) and transplant the rooted cuttings into small containers until they form roots before you move them to the garden.

Using cotton lavender

Although it is not used medicinally nowadays, Culpeper used to say of it: 'It resisteth poison, putrefaction, and heals the bitings of venemous beasts'. Today it is widely used as a moth-repellent and I have found it a powerful fishmoth-deterrent when placed in drawers and on bookcase shelves. It is a wonderful herb to add to potpourri mixtures (*see* p. 14) and sprigs can be placed in kennels and cat baskets to keep away fleas.

Planted in the garden, this herb will make an attractive border as well as a lovely accent plant amongst other shrubs.

In southern Europe this herb is used sparingly in cooking; at the most leaves are sprinkled on roast pork, added to tomato sauce, or simmered in stock.

❧ *White Satten groweth pretty well, so doth Lavender-Cotton.* ❧

John Josselyn

Cotton lavender

There are four varieties of cotton lavender:

S. chamaecyparissus

S. *chamaecyparissus*. A compact shrub growing to 40 cm/ 16 in. It lends itself to close clipping for a neat, low hedge for edgings or formal herb gardens. The grey leaves are dense and almost coral-like. The flowering is the same as S. *neopolitana* (below).

S. chamaecyparissus 'Nana'

This is a low-growing hybrid that is especially suitable for edging, rockeries or knot gardens.

S. neopolitana

This variety, with its feathery, loose, silky-grey foliage, grows to about 50 cm/20 in. It produces bunches of small, golden, composite buttons circled with minute flowers. It makes a lovely plant to introduce grey into the garden.

S. virens

This herb is about 60 cm/24 in height with green coral-like foliage, not quite as aromatic as the above varieties. It is, however, not readily available.

WORMWOOD

Artemisia absinthium

(Common broadleafed wormwood, absinthe)

This is an ancient herb of Europe, Asia and North America, originally known for its curative properties, but today used chiefly as a pest-deterrent. The specific name, *artemisia*, comes from two Greek words meaning 'devoid of delight', probably on account of its rank smell and extremely bitter taste.

The genus was named after Artemis, the Greek goddess of the hunt and the moon. Other sources claim that the genus *Artemisias* (over 200 mostly aromatic plants) was named after Artemisia, a famous botanist and medical researcher who was the wife and sister of the King of Caria, Mausolus. After his death in 353 BC, she took over the throne and built a magnificent tomb called the Mausoleum, one of the Seven Wonders of the ancient world, in his honour.

In olden days wormwood, together with anise, was an ingredient of a potent green liqueur named absinthe. The addition of this herb to absinthe is now illegal as it has a deleterious effect on eyes. Absinthe was popular with French impressionists, which, according to some, may account for the dotted effect manifest in some of their paintings.

The origin of the common English name is uncertain, but possibly has something to do with the fact that it was valued as a vermifuge, or expeller of intestinal worms.

❧ *A too habitual and free internal use of this herb dims the eyes for hours.* ❧

Culpeper

Growing wormwood

A shrubby perennial, liking full sun, aptly described in an old herbal as having 'leaves, large winged and divided into a great number of small parts, very much cut in; greenish above and hoary underneath'. Propagate by root division or cuttings (*see* p. 10).

Rain may wash toxins that inhibit growth from wormwood, so be sure not to plant this herb too close to medicinal or culinary herbs such as sage, fennel, anise or caraway. This herb will flourish in well-drained soil, with the plants spaced 0,6 m-1,8 m/2-4 ft apart. Take clippings in late summer.

❧ *What savour is best, if physic be true, for places infected than wormwood and rue?* ❧

Thomas Tusser

Using wormwood

Wormwood has a bitter, potent oil which is very volatile. Walk past a plant on a hot day and on licking your lips you will taste it. Wormwood can be grown around fruit trees to discourage coddling moth, or used in a dog's bath to remove and discourage the return of fleas. It is excellent in moth bags and hung dry in cupboards as a moth-deterrent.

The herb served in the past two centuries as a rather

vigorous diuretic for most urinary troubles; it was even believed to be a cure for a hangover, but being quite potent,
it must only be taken under medical supervision, if at all.

You can make your own effective organic insecticide to
use on mature plants to protect them against larger garden
pests such as moths and caterpillars as follows: Take 225 g/
8 oz of wormwood leaves and simmer in 2 ℓ/4 pt of water
for half an hour. Stir well, strain and leave to cool. Now
separately dissolve 5 ml/1 tsp of soap flakes or washing-up
liquid in 570 ml/1 pint of water. Mix with the wormwood
water and spray onto the troubled leaves as needed.

❝For the lips of a strange woman
drop as an honeycomb,
and her mouth is smoother than oil:
But her end is bitter as wormwood,
sharp as a two-edged sword❞

Proverbs

Wormwood

FENNEL

Foeniculum vulgare

(Wild liquorice)

The beautiful fennel is one of the oldest cultivated herbs used by the Chinese, Indians, Greeks, Romans and Egyptians for both medicinal and culinary purposes. Fennel was also listed among the nine sacred Anglo-Saxon herbs.

Up to the 16th century a wine known as 'sac' was made from fennel, rue and honey. This was gradually replaced by 'sack', a dry white wine from Spain.

Common fennel is a perennial growing to 2 m/6 ft 6 in with strong, smooth stems which have a pithy centre. The foliage consists of sprays of feathery, pale green leaves joined to the stem with pale brown clasping sheaths.

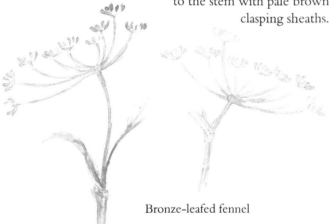

Bronze-leafed fennel

❧ *A farthyng-worth of fenel seed for fastying dayes.* ❧

Chaucer

The branching stems produce flattish heads of small yellow flowers which in turn become light brown, ribbed seeds. The bronze-leafed fennel is shorter in growth and with the bronzed foliage the flowers are more golden than yellow.

Growing fennel

Grown from seed, fennel will self-sow all too easily. If you want to transplant, you must do so when the plants are young as they become deep-rooted. Sow the seeds in an alkaline soil in a sunny position. Both common and Florentine fennel should be cut back to their base after flowering.

Fennel makes excellent food for small green caterpillars, so keep a watch out for them.

Green fennel is often found growing wild, but before you help yourself to some, make sure it has a strong smell of liquorice, that the stems and leaves are green and that the flowers are yellow; it just might be hemlock which is a deadly poison.

Using fennel

The leaves and seeds taste and smell of liquorice and aniseed, making it an excellent flavouring for a whole range of edibles. Fish, for instance, is delicious wrapped in mature leaves and placed over coals to cook. You can also mix young, lightly chopped leaves into sauces, salads, cottage cheese, potatoes and cooked eggs. The seeds, in turn can be added to pickling spices and, ground, are used to flavour apple pies, vegetable dishes, beetroot and carrot salads. The Romans were also known to cook the young shoots and serve them as a vegetable.

Medicinally, fennel was used by the Egyptians 'against all fevers' and the Greeks drank fennel tea as a slimming aid. To make a standard brew, take one teaspoon of seeds or one tablespoon of chopped, fresh leaves to a cup of boiling water. It is then taken three times a day for its diuretic properties and thus aids a slimming regimen. It is also said that chewing the seeds relieves hunger pangs.

Common fennel

❧ *Both the seeds, leaves and roots of fennel are much used in drinks and broths, for those that are grown fat, to abate their unwieldiness and to cause them to grow more gaunt and lank.* ❧

William Coles

FLORENTINE FENNEL

Foeniculum dulce

Florentine fennel is an annual known in Italy as 'finnochio'. It is shorter than other fennels and is mainly grown for its root which is white and bulbous, slowly growing to about the size of a tennis ball.

Growing Florentine fennel

Grow from seed sown in good soil, never allowing the ground to become too dry. As the root develops, it will appear above ground, when you must heap soil around it to keep it white and tender. Do not allow this fennel to flower as this impoverishes the root.

Using Florentine fennel

Wash and slice the root thinly and serve as a salad with a vinaigrette dressing or cook lightly in water, drain well and serve with a cheese sauce. The leaves may be used in the same way as other fennels.

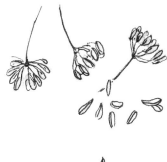

❧ *Above the lowly plants it towers,*
The fennel with its yellow flowers,
And in an earlier age than ours
Was gifted with the wondrous powers
Lost vision to restore. ❧

Henry Wadsworth Longfellow

SCENTED PELARGONIUMS

Pelargonium spp.

(Scented Geraniums)

Pelargoniums and geraniums are separate genera of the family Geraniaceae, but we nevertheless keep confusing the two and refer to all as geraniums, and I suppose they will always be known, grown and affectionately be called as such.

It is the strongly aromatic leaves of the pelargonium that have made it such a popular herb, and earned it the name of scented geranium. The word geranium is derived from the Greek *geranus*, meaning crane, which refers to the beaked fruit of the plant. The word pelargonium in turn comes from the Greek *pelargos*, which means a stork, and also refers to the slender stork bill-like fruit. Although the two genera grow differently, it seems that their fruit is similar.

There are about 250 species to be found from the Eastern Mediterranean to Southern Arabia, Canary Islands to Tristan da Cunha, and from India to New Zealand; though the greatest number are found in South Africa. Of these there are at least 50 listed scented variations. Pelargoniums only became popular in England in the last part of the 18th century and most of the hybrids grown in nurseries today stem from South African stock.

Variegated
rose-scented
pelargonium

The most commonly grown scented varieties are as follows:

P. radens (rose-scented)

This pelargonium grows in a shrub-like fashion to about 90 cm/25 in and is known by its fine yet deeply serrated green leaves. This herb and the one following are used as sources of commercial geranium oil.

P. graveolens (rose-scented)

The growth is similar to the variety described above, though it does attain heights of up to 1,5 m/4 ft 6 in. The leaves on this species are only moderately serrated. It will do well in dry conditions.

P. capitatum (rose-scented)

The serrations on this plant are shallow, yet the growth is as above. The flowers are pink with red-purple veins.

P. citriodorum (lemon-scented)

This herb is very upright, growing to about 60 cm/23 in. The leaves are stiff and rough and the many serrations come to points. It is bright green in colour.

P. crispum (lemon-scented)

produces light green, crisp, curled leaves and grows to a height of about 50 cm/20 in. This species also has a beautiful miniature variety that has tightly curled bright green leaves, about the size of a baby's fingernails.

P. x fragrans (nutmeg-scented)

This is a low-growing sub-shrub, with small, lightly serrated, grey-green leaves and the reputed scent of nutmeg, though I sometimes think it reminds more of camphor.

P. tomentosum (peppermint-scented)

This pelargonium has sprawling growth. I like to plant it where it gets shade and support from a shrub or a tree as in this way the large, dark green, velvety leaves are kept cleaner.

Remember that the scent of pelargoniums can vary with temperature, soil, season and personal sense of smell.

Growing pelargoniums

Most pelargoniums grow in full sun in average, well-drained soil, though the small addition of some bonemeal will improve the growth. All pelargoniums can be successfully planted in containers.

Propagation should be from cuttings (*see* p. 10) and I know of some people who dry their pelargonium cuttings for 24 hours before setting them in sand. The flowers of most of the scented varieties are very insignificant, ranging in colour from white to pink to mauve.

Using pelargoniums

Rose-scented pelargonium leaves are used fresh throughout the year to flavour stewed apples, pears, custards, puddings, rice, jellies and jams. When baking a cake for instance, place a couple of leaves in the bottom of the tin and pour the batter over. The leaves also make a good addition to a herb tea, but please, use with discretion at all times.

Lemon-scented geranium leaves also add wonderful flavour to soups, poultry, fish and teas.

If you have the peppermint variety in your pot or garden, try cooking the leaves with pears.

P. tomentosum

On a medicinal note, pelargonium leaves are effective as a poultice to draw septic sores and I believe a soft leaf tucked in the ear can relieve earache. A bath to which leaves have been added, will be helpful in alleviating general aches and pains. The rose-scented *P. graveolens* and *P. capitatum* are grown extensively for the extraction of rose oil.

On the whole, pelargonium leaves dry well, though the peppermint might take a little longer to become crisp. Their strong scent makes geranium leaves ideal for pot-pourri and herb pillows (*see* p. 15).

RUE

Ruta graveolens

(Serving men's joy, herb of grace)

The name 'rue' is taken from the Greek *reuo*, meaning to set free. It earned this name because of its alleged ability to cure so many ailments. For the same reason it was commonly called 'serving men's joy' by the Romans and Greeks who originally cultivated rue. They used it to cure, among others, a hangover and steeped it in their wine to prevent drunkenness.

The Pharisees included rue with mint as a tithe. It was said 'to banish evil spirits' and in Saxon times it had religious connotations, being known as the herb of grace. Included in herb posies and tussie mussies, it was said to ward off The Plague, and as a protection against jail fever, the herb was wound around the chairs of judges and other court officials. This was probably due to its very strong though not entirely unpleasant scent.

Growing rue

You would best propagate rue by sowing its seed or by striking cuttings (*see* p. 10) and, as someone said many years ago: 'better stolen from another man's garden' – meaning it self-sows easily and spreads from garden to garden.

Rue is a striking garden perennial with many divided lacy, grey-green leaves and soft, mustard-yellow flowers. The plant will grow to about 75 cm/30 in. It likes full sun and will even take dry conditions. Rue can be clipped to formal shapes, but if you're not that serious about the appearance of your garden, just see that the dead heads are removed and keep it well-clipped to prevent leggy growth.

There is a fine-leafed variety, 'Jackman's Blue', with distinctly blue-grey leaves that is quite freely available. I've been told that other hybrids are also known. Keep in mind that basil will not grow near rue. Also, a few people seem to be allergic to bergaptens, part of rue's chemical make-up, and when working with rue, on a hot day, can come out in blisters. If this is the case, immediately wash affected areas down with warm soapy water and rinse with cold water.

❦*A great preserver of chastity and preventer of lewd thoughts.*❧

Anon.

Common rue

Using rue

Some people use the herb in small quantities to flavour food. The Italian drink, Grappa, contains rue and in the Middle Ages it was often an ingredient of herb wines. Today it is sometimes added to flavour beer.

Imbibed in excess, rue may prove toxic and in the olden days Culpeper used to warn pregnant women not to take it at all. The presence of rutin in the herb is, however, said to strengthen tired blood vessels, especially in the eye, and to bestow second sight. Even Pliny agreed to this in his encyclopedic *Natural History*.

For the malady called lethargy, which is forgetfulness, take the herb rue, rinse it in vinegar and lay it on the brow.

Anon.

Jackman's Blue

INDEX

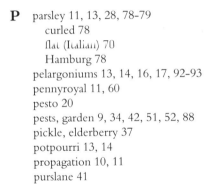